PRAISE FROM BUSINESS LEADERS FOR
COMMUNICATING WITH CUSTOMERS
AROUND THE WORLD

"A wealth of insights! Useful to anyone in international trade."
— Ed Artzt, Chairman of the Board & CEO, Procter & Gamble

"Very useful information for executives who meet with international customers, especially when the trips involve several countries in a matter of days." — Timothy J. Dwyer, Vice President, International, Sun Microsystems, Inc.

"This reference guide is 'must' reading for any manager or professional who needs to successfully communicate with international customers." — Karen Thomas, Group Manager, Sales Training, Sybase

"A wonderful resource from an experienced global manager. In two to four pages for each country, K. C. Chan-Herur provides the essential tips about communicating with international customers — and will save you from potential embarrassments." — Eric Kahn, Director, Consumer Product Development, VISA International

"Concise, practical & to-the-point. Exactly what a busy international business person needs! A perfect guide for your next international business meeting." — Helena Wong, Director, Business Development & Marketing, Pepsi-Cola International

"A gold mine of information . . . far more specific than other sources . . . organized in an easy-to-use manner."
— Edward F. McQuarrie, Ph.D., Marketing Professor, Santa Clara University; Author, *Customer Visits*

"Anyone expanding globally needs to explore a number of resources. This book is a good starting point on international business communication." — Alina ACE Aldape, Esq., President, The Americas Law Group

"A valuable resource with important information organized in a user-friendly, concise & easy-to-access format." — Pamela Monroe, President, 1993-1994, National Association of Women Business Owners, San Francisco Chapter; Principal, Monroe Associates

GLOBAL BUSINESS SERIES

COMMUNICATING WITH CUSTOMERS AROUND THE WORLD

A PRACTICAL GUIDE TO EFFECTIVE CROSS-CULTURAL BUSINESS COMMUNICATION

K. C. CHAN-HERUR

AUMONDE INTERNATIONAL PUBLISHING COMPANY
SAN FRANCISCO

Please address all inquiries to:
AuMonde International Publishing Company
P.O. Box 471705
San Francisco, CA 94147-1705
U.S.A.
Tel: 415. 281.8470
Fax: 415. 771.7731

Library Of Congress Catalog Card: 94-94276

ISBN: 1-885269-18-8

PRINTED IN THE UNITED STATES OF AMERICA

9 8 7 6 5 4 3 2

CONTENTS

For Vinod & Carolina

Acknowledgments

This book was inspired by a seminar my company developed for one of our clients & by international managers who wanted a practical guide to communicating with customers from around the world with their specific business needs in mind. It became a reality with the assistance & encouragement of many people. First, I'd like to thank Karen Thomas, who as Manager of Marketing Training & Development at Sun Microsystems, asked us to design a course on effective cross-cultural communication for international customer visits. I'm most grateful to Professor McQuarrie from Santa Clara University for sharing the market need for this reference book with me. I'd like to also thank Elaine Pratt, Al Lowe & Lew Jamison for the opportunity to be a part of the exciting & challenging partnership with SunU.

Many thanks to the audiences I have addressed at numerous corporations, professional organizations & universities for their enthusiasm on this book & on the broader topic of cross-cultural business communication. I'm also indebted to all the professionals whose work I have benefited from, many of whom are noted in the resource list of the book. Sincere gratitude to Ed Artzt, Chairman & CEO of Procter & Gamble, for offering me my first formal international marketing assignment at its Geneva, Switzerland's operation.

I'm also most appreciative for the encouragement, assistance & comments from many friends from around the world, especially: INSEAD Professor Linda Brimm, Jan & Paul Chaffee, Lai Hing Chan, José Chan, Pui Har & Woon Sun Chan, Dawson Church, Cynthia Dai, Claudio Engel, Peter Goodman, Jennifer Heggie, Sean Hockabout, H. & Ratna Hirannia, Eric Kahn, Anne Klein, Annabelle Lindo, Wharton Professor Len Lodish, Luz Marquez, Warren Moberly, Pamela Monroe, Luisa Pinto, Jim Prost, Margaret Pusch, M. Hélène Rit, Patricia Rojas, George Renwick, Gonzalo Sanchez, María José Sanchez, Linda Siddall, Helena Wong & Fran Zone.

To Carolina Keenan, who first "saw" this book. Your thoughtful suggestions & support were invaluable. Finally, to Vinod, my wonderful husband & partner for this & many other adventures. Thanks, merci & shukriar!

Preface

We all wish to have successful customer meetings. Since we are living in a global economy, many of those meetings will be with international customers in their home country or in the U.S. Over the last 25 years, I have had the pleasure & challenge of living and working cross-culturally in four continents. Given the opportunity to experience other cultures at work and in social situations, we can develop some well-tuned cultural antennas or a cultural "sixth sense."

But what about you, the busy executive and professionals who fly to Beijing, China, one week, then Santiago, Chile, the next and Riyadh, Saudi Arabia, the following week? You might have the good intentions of becoming familiar with the business protocols and communication norms of the countries you will soon visit, but when do you find the time? **This practical, concise and easy-to-use reference book is designed for you to use either at your office or to take along on your business trip.** Key business communication suggestions for each of the six major business regions and 33 countries have been summarized in a few pages, so that you can review the "must-know" information quickly before you leave your office, on the plane or in the hotel room at your international business destination.

Who can benefit from this book? Senior executives and managers, marketing mangers, sales, and engineering professionals, international managers and anyone who must communicate effectively with customers and business partners from around the world. These practical tips are also essential for meetings with international customers in the U.S.

I hope that you find this reference guide helpful and use it as a starting point. May you have many successful and profitable international meetings!

K. C. Chan-Herur
San Francisco, California
March 1994

I

GENERAL SUGGESTIONS SUMMARY

General Suggestions For Communicating With Customers Across Cultures

OBJECTIVE

This summary provides information that might be helpful to know during your customer meetings in an international location. **Its focus is on communication that is directly relevant to brief customer meetings and other communication situations**, rather than on the more complex preparation needed for longer stays involving negotiation and socializing. It will, however, provide useful tips relevant for those occasions, as well.

FOCUS

The summary provides a brief overview of relevant interactions in

GS

customer meetings in each of the major business regions around the world. These areas include:

- Language
- General Protocol & Information
- Introductions, Greetings & Business Cards
- Customer Meeting Schedules
- Communication During Customer Meetings
- Do's & Don'ts: Words & Gestures
- Gifts
- Other Useful Information

Where relevant, additional information about a particular country in that region is highlighted. Where no major differences exist, one of the above areas is omitted.

The **best way to use this Guide** is to read the **General Suggestions Summary**. Then read the information **on both the region and the country** you will be visiting. Certain key tips have been repeated intentionally in both the region and the country sections because they are important for you to know. Finally, review the **What To Know Before You Go** and the **International Customer Meeting Checklist** summaries in the Appendix.

Use these suggestions as a guide. Many of them are based on generalizations that are meant to be used as the **starting point** for your cross-cultural interactions. We hope that you will go beyond the surface to learn more about your international customers' culture, which will help develop more effective communication between your company and its international customer base.

Please **do** confirm with your local staff, business partners and other people involved in business communication that a specific suggestion is applicable for a particular customer or that part of their country. Today's global marketplace and business communication practices change quickly. In addition, individuals from the same country could react differently to the same behavior and conversation. Show respect towards your international customers. Keep an open and inquisitive mind. Learn from each interaction as you expand your cross-cultural communication skills.

We would appreciate it a great deal if you would send us your comments, suggestions or anecdotes. Your experience will help us enhance this Guide in the next edition.

We wish you many enjoyable and profitable cross-cultural customer meetings!

PRE-MEETING ACTION ITEMS
In addition to reviewing the *What To Know Before You Go* and the *Cross-Cultural Customer Meeting Checklist* summaries in the Appendix, remember to:

- Confirm at least two weeks in advance with both your local business contact and customers:
  - Meeting details (who you are meeting, date, time and location).

  - The agenda, the meeting objectives and expectations — in writing, if you haven't done so already.

- Send relevant written materials in advance, even if your customers speak English. Seeing the objectives and a few selected discussion items in writing or as a graphical representation could help make your meeting go smoother.

- Get an advance briefing on the customer and local business etiquette from your local contact or someone who is knowledgeable about the culture and country that you are going to visit. Anyone within or outside of your company who is from the targeted country or has done business there recently could be helpful.

LANGUAGE
While many of your customers speak English and you will probably be accompanied by someone who speaks the local language, you could create a great deal of goodwill if you try to say a few words, such

GS

as "excuse me, please and thank you" in the local language. You might find the summary of twelve key words with pronunciation keys for American-English speakers in the language section of the country helpful. For several of the major European languages (French, German, Italian and Spanish), the spelling of the words is included.

GENERAL PROTOCOL & INFORMATION

- Most people in countries around the world speak, act and dress more formally than people in the casual atmosphere that prevails at your company and in the U.S.

- Before your trip, meet with a couple of people you know who have recently been to the country you are about to visit. Find out additional information that will help minimize any *faux-pas* and make a good impression with your international customer. Also, ask the local staff or contact for a customer and business etiquette briefing, in advance or when you arrive.

- Observe local business partners and do as they do. When in doubt, ask your contact, mentor or host for the appropriate response.

- Avoid generalizing.

INTRODUCTIONS, GREETINGS & BUSINESS CARDS

- Ask your customer, "How would you like me to address you?" Err on the side of formality until you are asked to be on a first name basis, such as "Call me Bob." Find out the international customer's surname if it is not obvious to you. Hint: Many French-speaking countries write surnames in capital letters.

- Memorize a few of the key words, greetings and titles shown in the language section.

- Business cards are a "must." On the card, include your company name, your name, position and title. Include university degree(s) in Asia (especially India) and European countries (especially Russia). Avoid abbreviations. Have the reverse side of your business cards printed in the local language. In most of Southeast

Asia, Africa and the Middle East (except Israel), NEVER present your card or anything with your left hand.

* Give business cards to **everyone** in the meeting.

CUSTOMER MEETING SCHEDULES

* Avoid scheduling a business trip during Ramadan in Saudi Arabia, Carnival in Brazil, or Chinese New Year in China and other holy days for your business partners. Would you want to go to a business meeting on Christmas or other special holiday?

* Since the time and financial investment required for conducting customer meetings outside of your home country is even greater than for a domestic visit, it is important that you send a confirmation letter and an agenda in advance. Thus, your customers can prepare in those areas for discussion and you can reap maximum benefits from the meeting.

* Many countries use the 24-hour clock to schedule events, e.g., 4 p.m. is 16.00. The business week is Monday to Friday, unless otherwise noted.

COMMUNICATION DURING CUSTOMER MEETINGS

* The way we communicate is influenced a great deal by the culture in which we grew up. The ability to create rapport and to probe are two skills that are even more crucial when communicating with international customers. Since most of the people we meet in cross-cultural business meetings probably grew up in a culture quite different from ours, ways of creating rapport and probing can differ a great deal around the world.

* For example, in the U.S., one of the ways to create rapport and to show sincerity is to make direct eye contact throughout the conversation. In many countries in Asia, however, making direct eye contact is considered disrespectful and most Asians have been conditioned to avoid looking at their conversation partner. People who grew up in the U.S. might interpret lack of eye contact as disrespectful and not trust their customer or business partner.

GS

- Listening between the lines involves understanding relevant **nonverbal communication** signals, such as **physical distance** and other body language, as well as the notion of how **time** is viewed.
- Because family ties are especially important to Eastern cultures, you might consider mentioning your family life to show your stability as a business partner.

- Avoid asking "or" questions... you might get the answer "both" or "yes." Choices are not common in conversations. Due to customs or to the language barrier, your customers might take a longer time to think before answering your questions. Allow more time for silence and try not to stare at them while they are thinking. In many parts of the world, silence is highly valued.

- Speak slower and avoid using slang or acronyms that might be unfamiliar to your customers.

- Plan to ask only half as many questions as you would in the U.S., due to time needed for translation and other language needs. Meet with your interpreter in advance to brief him/her on the objective and agenda of the customer meeting.

- During formal presentations and informal conversation, especially for women who outrank any men present, avoid using "I." Instead, use "At our firm, we approach....," or "We decided to introduce...."

- For people from the U.S., it is important to remember that bigger, smarter and faster do not necessarily mean better everywhere.

DO'S & DON'TS: WORDS & GESTURES
- For most countries, it is best to avoid discussing politics, religion and social conditions.

- Where appropriate, certain gestures that might come up during a customer meeting will be noted. They are meant to help you understand better what your customer is saying. It is best to confirm the meaning of such gestures with him or her and to avoid using it yourself unless you are sure that you have all of the correct movements!

- Avoid the U.S. OK sign.

GIFTS
- Pens are considered safe gifts. Items with small logos from your company are usually acceptable.

OTHER USEFUL INFORMATION
- Read about the **culture and history** of the country you plan to visit for a customer meeting.   You might find some of the resources listed at the end of this book helpful.

- If invited out to a **meal**, the best response is to accept and eat whatever is offered, as it is usually equated to acceptance of host, country and company.   Your hosts will be flattered that you follow their lead.

- In most Latin America countries, as well as Italy, Spain and France, lunch is the biggest meal of the day and can last two to three hours.

- **Shoes** are forbidden within Muslim mosques and Buddhist temples. Never wear them into Japanese homes or restaurants. In Indian and Indonesian homes, if the host goes shoeless, do likewise.

- Take **time to rest** and sleep. Cross-cultural customer meetings usually require even more of your energy and attention than home country meetings.

For **women** in international business:
- In most countries, business is still conducted mostly by men.

- Consider using Mrs., even if you don't in the U.S. Mention your husband and children and ask about your hosts' families.

- A firm "NO" is advisable to undesirable advances, be it from strangers or business acquaintances.

II

REGION &
COUNTRY
SUMMARY

1

ASIA

GENERAL PROTOCOL & INFORMATION
- **Politeness** is most common and appreciated. **Group harmony** precedes personal feelings and ambitions. **Family** is of great importance.

- **Humility** or self-demeaning comments are normal in describing self or own accomplishments. Thus, praise is commonly denied.

- Don't say or do anything that will cause anyone to lose **face**... it will shame that person and you, the offender. It represents a breach of social courtesy. Saving face is to avoid embarrassment, failure, defeat or contradictions.

- Personal **relationship** is valued a great deal and is developed over a long period of time.

- Be especially respectful of **elders.**

- **Confucius'** philosophy continues to influence social and family relationship in all Chinese cultures, including those in China, Hong Kong, Taiwan and Singapore. That philosophy includes respect for authority, the natural order of things, and excelling within such order.

- Be **punctual** but don't be upset if your host is not.

- Be **patient**; decision-making tends to take longer than it might in the U.S.

INTRODUCTIONS, GREETINGS & BUSINESS CARDS
- In most of the Asian countries discussed, with the exception of Japan and India, handshakes and the use of Mr. or Mrs. before the surname are common in international business. But the locals have preferred, traditional ways of greeting and introduction, and some of them are shown below. Usually a nod or bow is appropriate between men and women.

- Have your business card ready and printed in the local language. University degrees are often included on the cards.

- Don't write on or bend anyone's business card.

CUSTOMER MEETING SCHEDULES
- Make appointments well in advance. Have a third party introduce you, stating your position and credentials in the introduction. Be punctual, but don't be offended if the customer arrives late.

SEATING ARRANGEMENTS
- Japan has the most elaborate and strictest seating arrangements. In most countries, it is acceptable and appropriate to let your host lead the way (in seating and going through the door) and tell you where and when to sit.

COMMUNICATION DURING CUSTOMER MEETINGS
- Pay particular attention to nonverbal expressions. Sometimes the nonverbal expression is the more important one.

- It would be especially helpful to have at least one observer on the customer meeting team.

- Avoid asking **"or"** questions... you might get the answer "both." Choices are not common in conversations in this region of the world.

- Your customers in Asia might take more time to think before answering your questions.

- Most Asians do not like saying "no" to anyone in person. They will probably say "it will be very difficult" or, if pressed, say "yes," meaning not "I agree," but "I understand."

- Always give your partner a chance to **save face**, to have a way out.

- Brief social talk, accompanied by tea or other beverages, precedes the business meeting, especially in Southeast Asia. Outward expression of opinions or feelings is rare.

- Avoid talking about religion, politics and poverty in your host's country.

GIFTS
- Small gifts are most appropriate and appreciated.

- When offered a gift, say thank you and offer some token resistance before accepting it with both hands.

- Gifts are generally not opened in the giver's presence.

CHINA
(People's Republic of)

1

LANGUAGE & KEY WORDS*

English	Chinese (Mandarin Pronunciation)
Good day	Něe hǒw
How are you?	Něe hǒw ma
Very well	Hǔn hǒw
Happy to meet you	Jǒ yǎhng dà míng
Goodbye	Dz'ài j'yèn
Mr.	Sh'yēn-shūng
Mrs.	Tài-tai
Yes	Shìh
No	Bòo shìh
Excuse me	D'wày bòo chěe
Please	Chǐng
Thank you	Sh'yèh-sh'yèh něe

- Pronunciation tips:
  - - = a flat tone
  - ´ = tone starts low and rises
  - ˇ = tone starts high, falls and then rises
  - ` = tone starts high and falls

- Chinese is traditionally written vertically from top to bottom and read right to left (backward from the Western perspective).

* Source and adaptation for Key Words shown here and those shown in other languages: *Around the World with 80 Words*, Charles Berlitz, Putnam Publishing Group, New York, 1991.

INTRODUCTIONS, GREETINGS & BUSINESS CARDS

• A slight bow is the traditionally appropriate way to greet each other. Chinese tend to be formal and reserved.

• Be very sensitive to your partner's title and status. Chinese often use the visitors' full title during introductions.

• The family name or surname usually comes first. Call Lee Chun Wan, Mr. Lee.

• A common greeting is *Něe hǎo ma* (How are you?)

CUSTOMER MEETING SCHEDULES

• Common business hours are 8 a.m. to noon and 2 p.m. to 6 p.m. Monday through Friday and Saturday morning.

• Make appointments well in advance. Have a third party introduce you, stating your position and credentials in the introduction. Be punctual, but don't be offended if the customer arrives late.

SEATING ARRANGEMENTS

• It is acceptable and appropriate to defer to your host on when and where to sit.

COMMUNICATION DURING CUSTOMER MEETINGS

• Pay particular attention to nonverbal expressions. Sometimes the nonverbal expression is the more important one.

• It would be especially helpful to have at least one observer in the customer meeting team.

• Avoid asking "or" questions... you might get the answer "both." Choices are not common in conversations in this region of the world.

• Your customers in Asia might take more time to think before answering your questions.

1

- Most Chinese do not like saying "no" to anyone in person. They will probably say "it will be very difficult" or, if pressed, say "yes," meaning not "I agree" but "I understand."

- Always give your partner a chance to **save face**, to have a way out.

- Brief social talk accompanied by tea or other beverages, precedes the business meeting. Outward expression of opinions or feelings is rare.

- Avoid talking about religion, politics and poverty in your host's country.

- Good topics of conversation include differences between China and the West and advances made by the Chinese. Others are its history, tradition and cuisine.

DO'S & DON'TS: WORDS & GESTURES
- Avoid mentioning Taiwan. Do not criticize Chinese leadership and its human rights record.

- Avoid the numbers 4 or 14; they sound like "death." Many Chinese will most likely refuse to accept, for example, a license plate with those numbers. On the other hand, the number 8 is considered to be a very lucky number and is sought after for all purposes.

- Don't rush transactions. They usually take months to years, rather than days or weeks.

- If invited out to a meal, avoid discussing business directly, unless the topic is initiated by your host.

- Avoid touching people you don't know well. A smile is preferred over a pat on the back.

- Pointing with one finger is considered impolite. Use the open hand instead.

- Avoid blue and white. They are colors for mourning.

GIFTS
- Small gifts are most appropriate and appreciated.

- Do not give a clock. It reminds people of death and represents bad luck.

- Gifts of great value can cause embarrassment and are rarely accepted.

- When offered a gift, say thank you and offer some token resistance before accepting it with both hands.

- Gifts are generally not opened in the giver's presence.

OTHER USEFUL INFORMATION
- Chinese are proud people, as shown in their language — guo-yü (the country's language), and chung-guo hua (the central country language). Both suggest that China is the center and most important part of the world. In a sense, it is. Chinese is spoken by over a billion people: More people speak Chinese than any other language.

- Lining up is a foreign idea and not practiced in China. In some regions, people spit in public after clearing their throat.

- Read the section on Asia and General Suggestions.

1

HONG KONG

LANGUAGE & KEY WORDS

English	Chinese (Mandarin Pronunciation)
Good day	Něe hǒw
How are you?	Něe hǒw ma
Very well	Hǔn hǒw
Happy to meet you	Jǒ yǎhng dà míng
Goodbye	Dz'ài j'yèn
Mr.	Sh'yēn-shūng
Mrs.	Tài-tai
Yes	Shìh
No	Bòo shìh
Excuse me	D'wày bòo chěe
Please	Chǐng
Thank you	Sh'yèh-sh'yèh něe

- Pronunciation tips:
    - ⁻ = a flat tone
    - ´ = tone starts low and rises
    - ˇ = tone starts high, falls and then rises
    - ` = tone starts high and falls

- Chinese is traditionally written vertically from top to bottom and read right to left (backward from the Western perspective).

- In addition to Mandarin, a large number of Hong Kong residents speak Cantonese and English.

INTRODUCTIONS, GREETINGS & BUSINESS CARDS
- Shake hands upon greeting and leaving customers.

- The family name or surname usually comes first. Call Lee Chun Wan, Mr. Lee.

- A slight bow is the traditionally appropriate way to greet each other. Chinese tend to be formal and reserved.

- A common greeting is *Nĕe hăo ma* (How are you?)

CUSTOMER MEETING SCHEDULES
- Common business hours are 9 a.m. to 5 p.m. (Monday to Friday), 9 a.m. to 1 p.m. (Saturday).

- Make appointments well in advance. Have a third party introduce you, stating your position and credentials in the introduction. Be punctual, but don't be offended if the customer arrives late.

COMMUNICATION DURING CUSTOMER MEETINGS
- *Doe-jay* is thank you in Cantonese (a popular Chinese dialect). The Chinese love it when a foreigner can speak their language, but be aware of the pronunciation.

- Casual inquiries about health or business are good, polite conversation.

- Avoid talking about the political situation in China.

- Always give your partner a chance to **save face**, to have a way out.

- Brief social talk accompanied by tea or other beverages precede the business meeting. Outward expression of opinions or feelings is rare.

DO'S & DON'TS: WORDS & GESTURES
- Most Chinese sit with their hands in their lap and feet on the floor.

- Avoid winking at others. It is considered impolite and has bad connotations.

- Don't rush transactions. They usually take months to years, rather than days or weeks.

- If invited out to a meal, avoid discussing business directly, unless initiated by your host.

- Avoid touching people you don't know well. A smile is preferred over a pat on the back.

- Pointing with one finger is considered impolite. Use the open hand instead.

- Avoid blue and white. They are colors for mourning.

- Avoid the numbers 4 or 14; they sound like "death." Chinese will most likely refuse to accept, for example, a license plate with those numbers. On the other hand, the number 8 is most sought after, as it is considered to be a lucky number.

GIFTS
- Small gifts are most appropriate and appreciated. Gifts of great value can cause embarrassment and are rarely accepted.

- Do not give a clock. It reminds people of death and represents bad luck.

- When offered a gift, say thank you and offer some token resistance before accepting it with both hands.

- Gifts are exchanged during Chinese New Year (usually around February).

OTHER USEFUL INFORMATION
- Read the sections on Asia and General Suggestions.

INDIA

LANGUAGE & KEY WORDS

1

English	**Hindi** (Pronunciation)
Good day	na-ma-STEH
How are you?	ahp-KHAI-sah hay
Very well	ah-cha
Happy to meet you	keh KOO-shee'wee
Goodbye	Peer-meh-LEN-gay
Mr.	SHREE-man
Mrs.	SHREE-mat-tee
Yes	haa
No	na
Excuse me	Ma-ahf
Please	Kroo-PEH-ya
Thank you	Shoo-KREE-ya

GENERAL PROTOCOL & INFORMATION

- Indian people tend to be religious, family-oriented and philosophical.

- They are proud of India's rich heritage with its many architectural and artistic masterpieces.

- Simple material comfort, rich spiritual accomplishments, humility and self-denial are valued and respected.

- Overt expressions of gratitude are generally saved for real favors rather than routine courtesies. Usually, a positive response is expected for a favor asked.

- Fatalism, as well as tolerance and social harmony, are common due to the major religions in India and its diversity.

1

- Hindus don't eat beef. Cows are sacred there. Muslims don't eat pork and strict Muslims don't drink alcohol. Orthodox Sikhs wear a turban and don't smoke, eat beef or cut their hair.

INTRODUCTIONS, GREETINGS & BUSINESS CARDS
- Men may shake hands with each other.

- Most people greet you by saying *Namaste,* with their palms together at chest level and a head nod.

- Men should avoid touching women.

- Include university degrees after your name on your business cards.

- Many Indians don't use a surname. Others use the first letter of their home town as their first name and their given name as the equivalent of a surname, e.g. H. Hirannia.

CUSTOMER MEETING SCHEDULES
- Make appointments well in advance. Have a third party introduce you, stating your position and credentials in the introduction. Be punctual, but don't be offended if the customer arrives late.

- Common business hours are 9:30 a.m. to 1 p.m. and 2 p.m. to 5 p.m. Monday to Friday and Saturday mornings.

COMMUNICATION DURING CUSTOMER MEETINGS
- Good topics of conversation include cultural achievements, Indian traditions, other people and foreign countries.

- Avoid discussions of personal affairs and India's poverty, military expenditures and foreign aid.

DO'S & DON'TS: WORDS & GESTURES
- Use only your right hand to accept or pass anything, especially food. Indians usually eat with their **right** hand. The left hand is generally used for personal hygiene.

- Some Indians say yes by bobbing their head from side to side.

- Pointing with one finger is considered impolite. Use the open hand instead.

- Don't refer to Native Americans as "Indians" in front of some-one from India.

GIFTS
- When offered gifts or food, it is polite to offer some resistance before accepting.

OTHER USEFUL INFORMATION
- Read the sections on General Suggestions and Asia.

JAPAN

LANGUAGE & KEY WORDS

1

English	**Japanese** (Pronunciation)
Good day	ko-nee-chee-wa
How are you?	ee-ka ga-dess-ka
Very well	gen-kee dess
Happy to meet you	ha-jee-meh-ma-sh'teh
Goodbye	sa-yo-na-ra
Mr.	-san (after name)
Mrs.	-san (after name)
Yes	hai
No	ee-yeh
Excuse me	soo-mee-ma-sen
Please	doh-zo
Thank you	ah-ree-ga-toh

GENERAL PROTOCOL & INFORMATION

- Conformity, to be in harmony with the crowd, is a characteristic of the Japanese people.

- Decisions are usually made at the highest level but details are taken care of by lower level staff. The senior manager is there more to see who his company is doing business with. Form is frequently more significant than content in some meetings.

- Business can and does continue from day to night. As the saying among Japanese businessmen goes, "You get through to a man's soul at night." However, business is not discussed at the beginning of the first meetings. Plan for meetings to be at least twice as long they would be in the U.S. Women are not usually welcome to after-dinner entertainment at bars. If you are a woman, excuse yourself and be grateful for the chance to rest before the next day's meeting.

INTRODUCTIONS, GREETINGS & BUSINESS CARDS

- Handshakes are becoming more common, although the traditional bow from the waist is the most popular form of greeting among the Japanese. (Remember to avoid prolonged eye contact... it is impolite.)

- The proper bow is also done with your hands sliding straight down on the sides, with a stiff back and neck. The bow says: I respect your experience and wisdom. The bow can be very elaborate, depending on rank, age, etc. For most visitors, a simple bow will do. In fact, Japanese don't expect non-Japanese to bow.

- Add -*san* to the person surname. For example, Yamamoto-*san* is equivalent to Mr. Yamamoto. Don't use -san with your own name. A Japanese's first name is reserved for use only by family and close friends.

- During the first few minutes of a meeting, time is invested in getting to know you and how your status relates to their own. Such information is shared among those present and all other relevant people to agree on how to deal with you. Thus, business cards are exchanged and many cups of tea are served.

- Present **business cards** with **both hands** and make sure the type is facing the recipient and is right-side-up.

CUSTOMER MEETING SCHEDULES

- Make appointments well in advance. Have a third party introduce you, stating your position and credentials in the introduction. Be punctual, but don't be offended if the customer arrives late.

- Common business hours are 8 a.m. to 5 p.m., Monday to Friday. Some businesses are also open on Saturday mornings.

SEATING ARRANGEMENTS

- Japan has the most elaborate and strictest seating arrangement.

1

- Seating is a highly formalized activity with a great deal of meaning to the Japanese. Guests usually sit furthest away from the door (usually facing the door). When in doubt, ask where your host would like you to sit. Wait until the host sits or asks you to sit before sitting down.

COMMUNICATION DURING CUSTOMER MEETINGS

- For the Japanese, whose culture calls for putting on the best face, even in the worst situation, a smile, a nod and even a "yes" can simply be a reluctance to disappoint.

- A sucking of breath through the teeth and a "It is very difficult" most likely means "NO."

- Laughter might not indicate joy or amusement, but a sign of embarrassment.

- The classic okay sign in the U.S. (thumb and forefinger forming a circle with other fingers pointing up) means "money."

- It is common for many Japanese women to cover their mouth when smiling or giggling.

DO'S & DON'TS: WORDS & GESTURES

- Keep eye contact to a minimum. Most Japanese spend a great deal of time looking at their fingertips, desk tops and the floor while speaking and listening. Whereas Westerners consider good eye contact as a prerequisite to trust, most Asians, including the Japanese, view it as a lack of respect and a personal affront.

- Never shake hands or give a presentation with either hand in your pockets.

- Don't yawn or chew gum in public.

- Sit erect with both feet on the floor.

- Avoid talking about World War II.

GIFTS
- Gifts that are most welcome include food and drink, such as brandy or frozen steaks, and those given in multiples of two (good luck), but avoid four (it sounds like death). The Japanese are fascinated by things with English words on them.

- Gift should be gift-wrapped in gray, brown, blue or green (considered business colors), and without a bow. Japanese take their gift-wrapping seriously.

- If offered a gift, thank the person and wait for one or two more offers before accepting the gift with both hands.

OTHER USEFUL INFORMATION
- Read the sections on General Suggestions and Asia.

1

SINGAPORE

LANGUAGE
- English is an acceptable business language. Other major languages used include Chinese, Malay and Tamil.

GENERAL PROTOCOL & INFORMATION
- Western business practice is common, however, the Chinese ways still dominate.

INTRODUCTIONS, GREETINGS & BUSINESS CARDS
- Singapore is quite westernized due to the British influence. Handshakes are common, with a slight bow to the Chinese and elders.

- Greetings in English are quite acceptable, even though with three major Asian cultures dominant in Singapore, traditional greetings depend on nationality and age group.

- Chinese put their surname first. Malays don't use surnames, but add *bin* (son of) to their own name. Indians don't have surnames, but use the initial of their father's name.

- Relationship is important to business success.

CUSTOMER MEETING SCHEDULES
- Make appointments well in advance. Have a third party introduce you, stating your position and credentials in the introduction. Be punctual, but don't be offended if the customer arrives late.

- Common business hours are 8:30 a.m. to 4:30 p.m. (Monday to Friday), and to 12:30 p.m. (Saturday).

COMMUNICATION DURING CUSTOMER MEETINGS
- Acceptable topics of conversation include travel experiences, news of countries visited and economic advances in Singapore.

- Remember to help people save face.

- Hostility between Malays and Chinese exists.

DO'S & DON'TS: WORDS & GESTURES
- Show courtesy with a slight bow when entering, leaving or passing a group of people.

- Don't touch people's heads. Don't put the ankle of one leg onto the other knee. Don't point the bottom of your feet at others.

- It is inappropriate to hit the fist into a cupped hand. It is rude to do finger gestures, including pointing and forming the OK sign.

- Pointing with one finger is considered impolite. Use the open hand instead.

- Don't litter; there are harsh penalties for doing so.

- Don't make humorous remarks about the food being served.

OTHER USEFUL INFORMATION
- Read the sections on General Suggestions, Asia and China.

SOUTH KOREA

LANGUAGE & KEY WORDS

English	Korean (Pronunciation)
Good day	ahn-N'YAHNG-ha-SHIM-nee-ka
How are you?	ahd-da kay chee neh SHIM-nee-ka
Very well	jahl-ee-SUM-nee-ka
Happy to meet you	bahn-gahp-SUM-nee-da
Goodbye	ahn-n'yahng-hee-ka-SHIP-shee-o
Mr.	shee-wa-boo-yin (after name)
Mrs.	shee-wa-boo-yin (after name)
Yes	yeh
No	ahn-i-yo
Excuse me	jay song HAM-nee-da
Please	joo SHIP-shee-o
Thank you	goh-map-SUM-nee-da

GENERAL PROTOCOL & INFORMATION

- The business environment is characterized by entrepreneurial spirit, Confucius philosophy and Japanese management practices.

- Koreans have a highly structured society. Age and position are highly respected. Courtesy and modesty are very important.

INTRODUCTIONS, GREETINGS & BUSINESS CARDS

- Korean surnames come first.

- A slight bow, accompanied by handshakes with both hands (left hand may support or rest under the right forearm to show respect) or using only the right hand, is common among men.

- Women don't usually shake hands.

- Business cards are exchanged with both hands, after the handshake.

CUSTOMER MEETING SCHEDULES

- Make appointments well in advance. Have a third party introduce you, stating your position and credentials in the introduction. Be punctual, but don't be offended if the customer arrives late.

- Common business hours are 9 a.m. to 6 p.m.

COMMUNICATION DURING CUSTOMER MEETINGS

- Koreans appreciate recognition of their country's economic growth during the last two decades.

- Don't criticize, openly disagree, or behave abruptly with Koreans. Avoid appearing excessively proud of accomplishments.

- Save face and maintain harmony.

- Drink the beverages offered at the start of the meeting without comment.

DO'S & DON'TS: WORDS & GESTURES

- Pointing with one finger is considered impolite. Use the open hand instead.

- Avoid talking or laughing loudly. Koreans, especially women, cover their mouth while laughing.

- Use both hands to pass and receive objects.

GIFTS

- Small gifts are most appropriate and appreciated.

- When offered a gift, say thank you and offer some token resistance before accepting the gift with both hands.

- Gifts are generally not opened in the giver's presence.

OTHER USEFUL INFORMATION

- When embarrassed, Koreans might respond by laughing.

- Men go through doors first. Women help men with their coats.

- Younger Korean men sometimes hold hands or walk with a hand on a friend's shoulder; it is an expression of friendship.

- Blowing your nose in public is considered bad manners.

- Read the sections on General Suggestions and Asia.

TAIWAN

LANGUAGE & KEY WORDS

1

English	**Chinese** (Mandarin Pronunciation)
Good day	Něe hǒw
How are you?	Něe hǒw ma
Very well	Hǔn hǒw
Happy to meet you	Jǒ yǎhng dà míng
Goodbye	Dz'ài j'yèn
Mr.	Sh'yēn-shūng
Mrs.	Tài-tai
Yes	Shìh
No	Bòo shìh
Excuse me	D'wày bòo chěe
Please	Chǐng
Thank you	Sh'yèh-sh'yèh něe

- Pronunciation tips:
  - - = a flat tone
  - ´ = tone starts low and rises
  - ˇ = tone starts high, falls and then rises
  - ` = tone starts high and falls

- Chinese is traditionally written vertically from top to bottom and read right to left (backward from the Western perspective).

- Taiwanese is also commonly spoken.

INTRODUCTIONS, GREETINGS & BUSINESS CARDS
- A nod of the head is acceptable for the first meeting.

1

- Handshakes are common for acquaintances and close friends.

- George Tu Chin, should be called Mr. or Dr. Tu or George Tu to his friends. Also, some people have abbreviated their given name, for example, T.Y. Ling. Avoid asking what it stands for.

- A common greeting is *Něe hao ma* (How are you?)

CUSTOMER MEETING SCHEDULES
- Make appointments well in advance. Have a third party introduce you, stating your position and credentials in the introduction. Be punctual, but don't be offended if the customer arrives late.

- Common business hours are 9 a.m. to 5 p.m. (Monday to Friday), to 1 p.m. (Saturday).

COMMUNICATION DURING CUSTOMER MEETINGS
- Taiwanese tend to be reserved, quiet, refined and friendly.

- "No" can be signaled by shaking one's hand from side to side with the palm forward.

- While sitting, most Taiwanese place both hands in the lap.

- Taiwanese refers to themselves by pointing to their nose.

- It is polite to stand up when someone who is important or older enters.

DO'S & DON'TS: WORDS & GESTURES
- Don't admire an object too much or the host might feel obligated to present it as a gift.

- Avoid discussing mainland China.

- Blinking the eyes at someone is impolite.

- Pointing with one finger is considered impolite. Use the open hand instead.

GIFTS
- Give gifts or other objects with both hands.

- Small gifts are most appropriate and appreciated.

- When offered a gift, say thank you and offer some token resistance before accepting the gift with both hands.

- Gifts are generally not opened in the giver's presence.

- Thank you notes are expected and appreciated.

OTHER USEFUL INFORMATION
- Read the sections on General Suggestions, Asia and China.

1

2

EASTERN EUROPE

CZECH REPUBLIC & SLOVAKIA

LANGUAGE
- Czechs speak Czech and Slovaks speak Slovak. However, they are very similar and each group understands the other's language. Both languages are part of the Slavic language family, which includes Russian, Polish, Bulgarian and Serbo-Croatian. German is the most common second language for businesspeople. For the younger generation, English is the most common second language.

2

GENERAL PROTOCOL & INFORMATION
- The Czech and Slovak are proud of their cultural heritage.

- They are not "touchers" in social situations and especially not in business situations.

INTRODUCTIONS, GREETINGS & BUSINESS CARDS
- Shake hands with everyone in the meeting upon both arrival and departure.

- A common greeting is *Dobry Den* (Good Day) or How do you do? (*TEH-shee-mnye*). Thank you is pronounced DE-kwee.

CUSTOMER MEETING SCHEDULES
- Make appointments well in advance and be punctual. However, don't be surprised that upon arrival to a meeting, you find a message requesting that you wait for an hour or longer. Avoid scheduling appointments too close together, in case of delays.

- Common business hours are 9 a.m. to 5 p.m.

- Avoid meetings in July and August, most people vacation then.

- Telephone systems are not generally reliable and you might often not be able to make a call at a predetermined time to your customer until many hours later.

COMMUNICATION DURING CUSTOMER MEETINGS

- Sport is a good topic of conversation. Avoid discussing politics, religion and social conditions.

- Accept the drinks or coffee offered to you at the beginning of the meeting. If a toast is offered, offer one in return.

- Take proposals with a grain of salt. They might agree to do something, even if there is only a slight possibility of success or when they can't do something.

- To show that something or someone is crazy, Czechs and Slovaks "screw" a stiff forefinger into the temple of the head.

DO'S & DON'TS: WORDS & GESTURES

- For women: Feminine and nonagressive behaviors will be more effective with most people. International businesswomen can be successful as they are viewed as a novelty.

- Avoid talking about politics or religion.

GIFTS

- Take wine, whiskey or cognac, quality chocolates / candies and odd numbers of flowers (social).

OTHER USEFUL INFORMATION

- The former Czechoslovakia is now two distinct countries.

- Read the General Suggestions section.

2

HUNGARY

LANGUAGE & KEY WORDS

English	Hungarian (Pronunciation)
English	**Hungarian** (Pronunciation)
Good day	yo-NAW-pot
How are you?	hodj vawn?
Very well	yol VA-d'yok
Happy to meet you	UHR-ven-dek
Goodbye	VEE-sont-LA-tash-ra
Mr.	oor (after name)
Mrs.	nay (after name)
Yes	EE-ghen
No	nem
Excuse me	BO-cha-shon mehg
Please	KAY-rem
Thank you	KUH-suh-num

GENERAL PROTOCOL & INFORMATION

• Hungary is one of the most open and prosperous countries in Europe. Hungarians are very proud of their cultural heritage and political advances.

• Hungarians like their personal space and usually stand about an arm's length apart.

• Men usually walk to the left of women or other honored guests.

INTRODUCTIONS, GREETINGS & BUSINESS CARDS

• The common greeting is a handshake. The man usually waits for the woman to extend her hand first.

• Individuals are addressed by the last name, followed by the first name (e.g., Mr. Smith, Robert). Hungarian business cards are presented this way, unless they are printed in English.

CUSTOMER MEETING SCHEDULES
* Make appointments well in advance and be punctual.

* Common business hours are 8 a.m. to 6 p.m. (closed at lunch).

COMMUNICATION DURING CUSTOMER MEETINGS
* Hungarians are known to be pessimistic, even when things are going well. Don't be frightened away by dire predictions.

* Good topics of conversation include food, wine and what you like about Hungary.

DO'S & DON'TS: WORDS & GESTURES
* Avoid talking about politics or religion.

GIFTS
* Western liquor and flowers (except red roses) are acceptable for social situations.

OTHER USEFUL INFORMATION
* Hungary is the home of the famous Rubik's Cube. Hungarians tend to be highly educated and technically proficient.

* Read the General Suggestions section.

2

POLAND

LANGUAGE & KEY WORDS

English	Polish (Pronunciation)
Good day	dzhen-DOH-brih
How are you?	yahk sheh pahn MYEH-va/
	yahk sheh PA-nee-MYEH-va*
Very well	BAR-dzo DOHB-zheh
Happy to meet you	BAR-dzo mee MEE-woh
Goodbye	doh veed-ZEHN-ya
Mr.	pahn
Mrs.	PA-nee
Yes	tahk
No	nyeh
Excuse me	psheh-PRA-shahm PA-na
Please	PRO-sheh
Thank you	djen-KOO-yeh

* Masculine / feminine forms

GENERAL PROTOCOL & INFORMATION
- The Poles tend to be self-reliant and individualistic, as well as outgoing and outspoken.

- They are very proud of their cultural heritage and survival abilities.

INTRODUCTIONS, GREETINGS & BUSINESS CARDS
- Shake hands when you first meet and again when departing. Men usually wait for women to extend their hand first.

- Address your host by title and last name, such as Mr. Walesa.

CUSTOMER MEETING SCHEDULES
- Make appointments well in advance and be punctual.

- Common business hours are 8 a.m. to 6 p.m. (closed at lunch).

COMMUNICATION DURING CUSTOMER MEETINGS

- People usually stand about an arm's length from each other when conversing. There is usually no touching while speaking in business, except among close friends.

- Poles tend to speak softly. Good topics of conversation include Poland and its cultural history, life in your home country, your family and its activities.

- You might be offered cognac at business and other meetings. People in Poland enjoy hard liquor.

DO'S & DON'TS: WORDS & GESTURES

- A common gesture used in Poland to invite a close friend to have a vodka or other drinks is to flick one's finger against the neck. You might not want to use it, since it is considered rude unless you use this gesture with a close friend.

OTHER USEFUL INFORMATION

- Don't mention German or Russian involvement in World War II.

- Read the General Suggestions section.

2

RUSSIA

LANGUAGE & KEY WORDS

English	Russian (Pronunciation)
Good day	DOH-bree d'yen
How are you?	kahk vee pa-zhee-VA-yeh-t'yeh
Very well	OH-chen'ha-ra-SHO
Happy to meet you	OH-chen rahd/ OH-chen'ra-da*
Goodbye	da svee-DA-n'ya
Mr.	Gospodin
Mrs.	Gospozha
Yes	da
No	n'eyt
Excuse me	iz-vee-NEE-t'yeh
Please	pa-ZHAHL-sta
Thank you	spa-SEE-ba

* Masculine / feminine forms

GENERAL PROTOCOL & INFORMATION

• Fatalism, pessimism, conformity, as well as expansiveness, generosity and letting go are some of the Russian traits.

• Due to the past suppression of personal opinion, personal initiative and responsibility for oneself, even when Russians are happy, they are reluctant to show those feelings in public and tend to express frustration with daily life. But they are beginning to value open discussion, compromise, personal creativity and risk taking.

• Russians tend to have a good sense of humor.

INTRODUCTIONS, GREETINGS & BUSINESS CARDS

• Russians usually shake hands in the first meeting with a simple *DOH-bree d'yen'* (Good day) with direct eye contact.

- *Gospodin* Sarakov (Mr. Sarakov) is the formal business greeting. A step less formal is Boris Mikhail and the informal one is Boris. *Gospodin and Gospozha* (Mrs.) are being revived after Communism and people are still getting used to it.

- Business cards should be printed in Cyrillic and include university degrees. Give business cards to everyone in the meeting.

CUSTOMER MEETING SCHEDULES
- Make appointments well in advance and be punctual.

- Common business hours are 9 a.m. to 6 p.m. (closed at lunch).

COMMUNICATION DURING CUSTOMER MEETINGS
- Russians prefer to have social contact before discussing business. Mir (Peace) is a most popular subject.

- The common answer, out of habit, is "no" to any question. One needs to persist to get to the final answer. Here probing might be especially important.

- Shaking a raised fist indicates disagreement and anger. The "thumbs up" sign shows approval.

DO'S & DON'TS: WORDS & GESTURES
- Avoid talking about the negative aspects of Soviet or Russian history and its alcohol problem.

- Do turn and face people when you need to pass them, especially in an auditorium or theater.

- Avoid the OK sign; it might be interpreted by some people as vulgar.

- Never cut into a line. Long and orderly lines of people are common in Russian daily life.

GIFTS
- Russians enjoy printed T-shirts, caps (with company logo), jeans and almost anything from the U.S. Other favorite gifts from international guests include food and books.

OTHER USEFUL INFORMATION
- Russians tend to be more expressive and freer to share their real opinion when they are in a small and familiar group.

2

3

Western Europe

GENERAL PROTOCOL & INFORMATION

- Behave as if you are visiting a rich old relative and mind your manners. Speak and dress more formally. Jackets usually stay on in offices, restaurants and on the street.

- Cardinal sins include gum chewing, yawning without covering one's mouth, back slapping, as well as talking with hands in pockets and legs propped up on furniture.

INTRODUCTIONS, GREETINGS & BUSINESS CARDS

- Avoid using first names unless told to do so. Call your international customers by their academic titles, e. g. *Doktor Braun*, better yet *Herr Doktor Braun*.

- A handshake is the standard greeting but it is done with a limper squeeze than the firm and strong handshake favored by U.S. businesspeople. Shake hands with both men and women.

- Business cards are a must.

- Punctuality is a must (especially in Switzerland, the Netherlands and Germany), except in some southern European countries such as Greece and Spain.

CUSTOMER MEETING SCHEDULES

- Make appointments well in advance. Punctuality is valued.

- Avoid July and August, Holy Week (around Easter) and the last half of December. Check with the local staff or sales representative to make sure that you don't schedule the meeting on or around a local holiday.

COMMUNICATION DURING CUSTOMER MEETINGS

- Both verbal and nonverbal communication tends to be more formal.

- It is polite and expected that people sit straight with knees together or legs crossed at the knee. Feet are not to be placed on tables or chairs.

- Don't speak with your hands in your pockets.

DO'S & DON'TS: WORDS & GESTURES

- Casualness is equated with rudeness, so sit up straight and don't put your feet on tables or chairs.

- Pulling an eyelid means "Be alert" or "I am alert."

- Don't talk with something in your mouth.

- Cover your mouth when yawning.

- Use handkerchiefs discreetly.

GIFTS

- Gifts are not generally expected. However, if you wish to give a gift, in addition to your company gifts, other suggestions follow.

- If a need for a social gift arises, chocolates and flowers (note the appropriate numbers and the ones to avoid) are usually acceptable. Chrysanthemums (associated with death) and red roses (associated with romantic love) should be avoided.

BELGIUM

LANGUAGE
- Belgium has two official languages, Dutch and French .

- The Walloons speak French and the Flemings speak Flemish (Dutch). In Brussels, visitors should speak English or French, even though it is in the Flemish side of the country. If you are not sure if a Belgian speaks French or Flemish, speak to him or her in English. Don't speak French to a Fleming or Flemish to a Walloon.

- See key words in French and Dutch in the France or Netherlands section, respectively.

GENERAL PROTOCOL & INFORMATION
- Belgians tend to be deductive and pragmatic.

- In general, Belgians have a good sense of humor and can usually laugh at themselves. Avoid telling jokes; they don't translate well.

- Privacy is highly valued and respected.

INTRODUCTIONS, GREETINGS & BUSINESS CARDS
- Address business partners by last name or title. A quick and light handshake is used to greet and to say goodbye to each person at business and social gatherings. Men wait for the women to extend their hand first.

CUSTOMER MEETING SCHEDULES
- Make appointments well in advance. Punctuality is valued.

- Arriving more than 30 minutes late is considered rude.

- Common business hours are 9 a.m. to 6 p.m.

COMMUNICATION DURING CUSTOMER MEETINGS

- The Walloons (French side) tend to be warmer and more expressive, while the Flemings tend to be more reserved.

- Good topics of conversation include sports, popular books, as well as Belgian cultural heritage, especially art and architecture. Belgians are very proud of their culture. Topics to be avoided include personal matters, politics, local language differences (French vs. Flemish) and religion. Belgians often tell jokes about the Dutch and vice versa. Stay out of such rivalry.

DO'S & DON'TS: WORDS & GESTURES

- Don't snap your fingers. Avoid back-slapping and being noisy.

- Men allow women to enter rooms first and also rise when women enter a room.

- Avoid pointing with the index finger, scratching and yawning.

GIFTS

- A recent book related to their industry would be welcome.

- Don't send chrysanthemums. They are associated with death.

OTHER USEFUL INFORMATION

- Around Antwerp (mostly Flemish and, therefore, Dutch), you will probably find more order and efficiency in how things get done. Around Brussels (mostly Walloons and, hence, French), you will find more French features, including more three-star restaurants.

- See Western Europe and General Suggestions sections.

DENMARK

LANGUAGE & KEY WORDS

English	**Danish**(Pronunciation)
Good day	goo-day
How are you?	vorh-DAHN hahr dee deh
Very well	MAY-et goth
Happy to meet you	deh var mor-SAHMT
Goodbye	fahr-VEHL
Mr.	HEHR
Mrs.	FROO
Yes	ya
No	nay
Excuse me	OON-skewl my
Please	vehr VEHN-lee
Thank you	tahk

3

GENERAL PROTOCOL & INFORMATION

- Danes tend to be informal and friendly. Proper etiquette is important and courtesy is most appreciated.

- Denmark has a high standard of living and a high tax rate. The Danes are proud to take responsibility for their nation's welfare.

- They tend to be tolerant of diversity in people and points of view.

INTRODUCTIONS, GREETINGS & BUSINESS CARDS
- A firm and brief handshake is most common.

CUSTOMER MEETING SCHEDULES
- Common business hours are 8 a.m. to 4 or 5 p.m.

- Avoid conducting heavy business in July and August. Danes like to enjoy their summer months, as most Scandinavians do.

- Be punctual.

COMMUNICATION DURING CUSTOMER MEETINGS
• During conversations, eye contact is important but the Danes rarely use hand gestures.

DO'S & DON'TS: WORDS & GESTURES
• Politeness is most important.

• To most Danish women, equality is very important. Nonetheless, traditionally, women go through doors first. Men should allow their host to hold the door for them. Gentlemen go up stairways first, but ladies come down the stairs first.

OTHER USEFUL INFORMATION
• There is no tipping on restaurant and hotel bills or for taxi fares.

• Flowers are acceptable as gifts for social occasions.

• If you go out with the Danes, they might surprise you with their potent aquavit ("water of life").

• Formal dinners are quite common. If you are planning to attend, bring your formal wear.

• See Western Europe and General Suggestions sections.

3

FRANCE

LANGUAGE & KEY WORDS

English	French	Pronunciation
Good day	Bonjour	bohñ-ZHOOR
How are you?	Comment allez -vous?	kohm-mawñ tahl-la -VOUS
Very well	Très bien	tray B'YEÑ
Happy to meet you	Enchanté	ahñ-shawñ-TAY
Goodbye	Au revoir	o ruh-VWAHR
Mr.	Monsieur	muh-s'YERR
Mrs.	Madame	ma-DAHM
Yes	Oui	wee
No	Non	nohñ
Excuse me	Pardon	par-DOHÑ
Please	S'il vous plaît	seel-voo-PLAY
Thank you	Merci	mehr-SEE

Note: ñ represents a nasal n produced through the nose. zh is pronounced as the s in pleasure.

3

GENERAL PROTOCOL & INFORMATION

- The French tend to measure success by education level, school attended, family reputation and financial status.

- They are patriotic and extremely proud of their culture, heritage and nation.

- They tend to be reserved and private. People outside of Paris are likely to be more hospitable.

- The French believe that there is more to life than their job. People work hard but don't admire workaholics. Weekends are for family, culture and relaxation. Vacations are sacred; most take the entire month of August off.

INTRODUCTIONS, GREETINGS & BUSINESS CARDS

• The French shake hands both upon meeting and when departing. Their handshake is a light grip and a single quick shake. As a general rule, French women offer their hands first, if they want to shake hands.

• In offices, people shake hands with everyone in the room, even if it takes 15 minutes daily. They appreciate personal contact and relationship.

CUSTOMER MEETING SCHEDULES

• Make appointments well in advance. Punctuality is valued.

• Avoid July and August; most French people take their vacation then.

• Common business hours are 9:30 a.m. to 6:30 p.m.

• Avoid scheduling meetings before 9:30 a.m., as most people don't start their work until then.

COMMUNICATION DURING CUSTOMER MEETINGS

• The French tend to get down to business quickly, but are slow to come to decisions and are fascinated by details.

• Show respect and appreciation for French cuisine, art and history. The French are pleasantly impressed if you can talk about them.

• They enjoy innovation and gadgets, wherever they might come from.

• The famous Gaelic shoulder shrug with palms extended means "it doesn't worry me." If the palms are raised to chest level, it means "What do you expect me to do about it?"

• The classic okay sign in the U.S. (thumb and forefinger forming a circle with other fingers pointing up), means "zero" or "worthless" in France.

3

DO'S & DON'TS: WORDS & GESTURES

- Avoid personal questions, politics and money during conversations.

- The French love an argument and can become quite heated during the discussion. After it is over, they are calm again and might even say, "Let's do that again soon."

- Avoid slapping an open palm over a closed fist. It is considered vulgar.

- Playing an imaginary flute is a way of indicating that someone is talking on and on and is become tiring.

GIFTS

- Avoid gifts with a large company name or logo. Gifts appealing to the intellect or aesthetics are most appreciated.

- Don't give a French person wine as a gift, unless you are certain of its high quality.

- If you send flowers for social occasions, avoid roses and chrysanthemums.

OTHER USEFUL INFORMATION

- See the Western Europe and General Suggestions sections.

3

GERMANY

LANGUAGE & KEY WORDS

English	German	Pronunciation
Good day	Guten Tag	GOOT'en tahk
How are you?	Wie geht's?	vee gehts
Very well	Sehr gut	zair goot
Happy to meet you	Sehr erfreut	zair air-FROYT
Goodbye	Auf Wiedersehen	owf VEE-dair-zay'n
Mr.	Herr	hair
Mrs.	Frau	frow
Yes	Ja	ya
No	Nein	nine
Excuse me	Verzeihung	fair-TS'EYE-oong
Please	Bitte	BIT-teh
Thank you	Danke schön	DAH-keh shern

3

GENERAL PROTOCOL & INFORMATION

- Most Germans tend to be quite business-oriented, but have a clear separation of work and private lives. Germans also tend to be competitive, ambitious, hardworking, orderly, well-educated, well-traveled and well-informed.

- Individual success is important and measured by the car Germans drive, the size of their office and where they go on vacation.

- They are impressed by people who can relate to their classical education, including music, history and art.

- Gentlemen walk and sit to the left of all ladies and men of senior business rank. But on busy streets, men walk on the side where traffic is passing.

INTRODUCTIONS, GREETINGS & BUSINESS CARDS

- Don't shake hands all at once when you are in a group, as it is inappropriate to cross someone else's handshake. Be sure to address people with all the appropriate titles in addition to Mr., for example, *Herr Doktor Braun* (Mr. Dr. Braun).

CUSTOMER MEETING SCHEDULES
- Make appointments well in advance. Punctuality is highly valued.

- Common business hours are 8 a.m. to 5 p.m.

COMMUNICATION DURING CUSTOMER MEETINGS
- It is polite to remain standing until offered a seat, as well as to stand when a woman enters the room.

- Germans appreciate intelligent conversations, but could become critical of certain ideas. Good topics of conversation include the German countryside, hobbies and sports such as soccer.

- Germans tend to be more status conscious and more formal than most people in the U.S.

- They tend to be pessimistic and have a tendency to tell why something can't be done before saying why it can succeed.

DO'S & DON'TS: WORDS & GESTURES
- Avoid references to baseball, basketball or American football.

- Germans greet and say good-bye with each other by rapping their knuckles lightly on the table, if there is a large party in the room. This gesture is also used by university students when greeting their professors.

- A raised, clasped hand is often used to signal "thanks" to a group of people.

- To signal for silence, put your index finger over your lips, with the fingernail facing outward.

- Hold the thumb upright to indicate "one."

3

- It is very rude to point the index finger to the temple and make a screwing motion. Some Germans use it to express their unhappiness with someone and it means "You are crazy!"

- "Good Luck" is shown by lightly pounding two fists with thumbs tucked inside the other fingers.

GIFTS
- Avoid giving red roses (symbols of love) or carnations (symbol of mourning). In any case, unwrap flowers before you present them.

OTHER USEFUL INFORMATION
- Men enter a restaurant first because, according to custom, the man must inspect the restaurant to make sure that it is proper for a woman to enter.

- There is quite a bit of tension between Germans from the West and the East. Easterners feel that they are treated as second-class citizens; Westerners resent the economic burden of rebuilding the East.

- See Western Europe and General Suggestions sections.

3

GREECE

LANGUAGE & KEY WORDS

English	**Greek** (Pronunciation)
Good day	ka-lee-MEH-ra
How are you?	pohs EES-theh
Very well	po-LEE ka-LA
Happy to meet you	HEH-ro po LEE
Goodbye	ah-DEE-oh
Mr.	KEE-ree-os
Mrs.	kee-REE-ya
Yes	nay
No	OH-hee
Excuse me	meh seen-ho-REE-teh
Please	pa-ra-ka-LO
Thank you	ef-ha-ree-STO

3

GENERAL PROTOCOL & INFORMATION

- The Greek respect the elderly and address them with courteous titles. The elderly have a great deal of authority.

- Greeks also value personal contact, individual responsibility, and collectivism.

- Greek hospitality tends to be sincere and generous (even over-whelming, at times).

INTRODUCTIONS, GREETINGS & BUSINESS CARDS

- There are no rules of greeting. Greeks may shake hands, embrace and/or kiss at the first and every meeting. For visitors, a firm handshake and good eye-contact is recommended.

- Any attempt to address them in Greek will be appreciated. Use *Kyrie* (KEE-ree-os) or *Kyria* (kee-REE-ya), which can be used with the first and last name or by itself. Greeks tend to be informal soon after meeting you and will probably ask you to use their first name, even before you ask.

CUSTOMER MEETING SCHEDULES
- Common business hours vary, but mostly are 8 a.m. to 1:30 p.m. and 5 to 8 p.m.

- Punctuality is less important here, but it is best to be there on time and wait for your host.

COMMUNICATION DURING CUSTOMER MEETINGS
- Greeks tend to be very expressive, both verbally and with body language. To most outsiders, a normal exchange could be mistakenly viewed as a full-blown argument. Chances are something is wrong if your host becomes quiet and withdrawn.

- Pretentiousness and standoffishness aren't appreciated.

- Greeks prefer to express themselves orally and quite strongly. In fact, they generally dislike written documents, including agendas or memos and will probably question the necessity of having the information on permanent file.

- Avoid talking about Cyprus and any international controversies involving Greece.

- "No" is shown by nodding slightly upward (the "yes" gesture in the U.S.). "Yes" or "of course" is shown by tilting the head to either side. Also, to indicate "OK," use the "thumb's up" gesture.

- A smile could mean happiness and satisfaction or intense anger.

- When complimented, a Greek might issue a puff of air through pursed lips to ward off the "evil eye" (an old custom).

DO'S & DON'TS: WORDS & GESTURES
- Waving your whole hand is an insult, but it means "no" in most European countries and "good-bye" in the U.S.

• Do not use the U.S. "OK" sign or the fig gesture (a clenched fist with the index finger over the protruding thumb between the knuckle of the index and middle fingers), as they are considered obscene.

OTHER USEFUL INFORMATION

• Many people casually finger "worry beads" to release nervous energy, rather than for any religious meaning. This is quite common in the Middle East and Mediterranean area.

• See Western Europe and General Suggestions sections.

3

ITALY

LANGUAGE & KEY WORDS

English	Italian	Pronunciation
Good day	Buon giorno	bwohn JOR-no
How are you?	Come sta?	KO-meh sta
Very well	Benissimo	beh-NEE-see-mo
Happy to meet you	Piacere	p'ya-CHEH-reh
Goodbye	Arrivederci	ah-ree-veh DEHR-chee
Mr.	Signore	seen-YO-reh
Mrs.	Signora	seen-YO-ra
Yes	Sì	see
No	No	no
Excuse me	Scusi	SCOO-zee
Please	Per piacere	pehr p'ya-CHEH-reh
Thank you	Grazie	GRA-ts'yeh

3

GENERAL PROTOCOL & INFORMATION

- Italians tend to be very open, curious and tolerant of other ways of behavior. They have a high tolerance for inefficiency and genuine mistakes but low tolerance for arrogance and rudeness.

- Southern Italians enjoy a leisurely life and pace of doing business, while Northern Italians feel pressured and are jealous of their time. There are some tensions between northerners and southerners due to their different priorities and economic conditions.

- Italian business relationships are based on interdependence and mutual obligation, which often are satisfied by members of the extended family. Most successful organizations in Italy are owned by a family or modeled after the family.

- Relationship is most important. Once the players in the relationship see where everyone can benefit, cooperation and commitment are assured.

INTRODUCTIONS, GREETINGS & BUSINESS CARDS
- Shake hands when meeting and leaving, regardless of how brief the meeting was or how often you meet. Guests are always introduced first.

- All university graduates have a title and usually expect to be addressed as *dottore* (liberal arts), *avvocato* (law), *ingegnere* (technical field) and *professore* (professors and most medical doctors).

CUSTOMER MEETING SCHEDULES
- Common business hours are 9 a.m. to 1 p.m. and 3 to 7 p.m.

- It is impolite to arrive to a meeting late (beyond 20 minutes is rude), but it is even more impolite to break a meeting that is running over. Thus, if something unexpected comes up that causes an Italian to be late, most people would understand. So allow extra meeting time.

COMMUNICATION DURING CUSTOMER MEETINGS
- It might be challenging to stick to the agenda, as most meetings tend to be unstructured and informal.

- Common topics of discussion include soccer, family affairs, business and local news. Avoid talking about American football and politics.

- Italians often use hand gestures during conversations, especially in the South.
    - A common gesture of rubbing the thumb rapidly against the fingers indicates money.
    - A shoulder shrug means "I don't know" or "I don't care."
    - A finger pushing down slightly under the eye means someone is smart or clever.
    - A raised fist with index and little fingers extended means that someone is being cuckolded. (Wife is being unfaithful.)

3

DO'S & DON'TS: WORDS & GESTURES
•   A nose tap means a friendly warning.

•   A chin flick means " Not interested" or "Buzz off."

•   It is ungracious to refuse an insistent invitation for lunch or dinner. Lunch is the biggest meal of the day and could last two to three hours.

•   Men do remove their hats when entering buildings.

GIFTS
•   An exchange of business gifts is common.

•   For social gifts, avoid giving chrysanthemums; take an odd number of flowers.

OTHER USEFUL INFORMATION
•   Italians are among the most demonstrative people in the world. That is reflected in their social greeting, conversation and all of their relationships.

•   It is common and acceptable for two Italian men or women to walk together arm-in-arm.

•   Telephone service is not always reliable and, thus, is not used extensively.

•   See Western Europe and General Suggestions sections.

3

NETHERLANDS

LANGUAGE & KEY WORDS

English	Dutch (Pronunciation)
Good day	KHOO-den dakh
How are you?	hoo khaht ut
Very well	hayl ghoot
Happy to meet you	PRET-tukh ü tuh awnt-MOO-tuhn
Goodbye	dakh
Mr.	muh-NAYR
Mrs.	muh-FROW
Yes	yah
No	Nay
Excuse me	par-DAWN
Please	ahl-stü-BLEEFT
Thank you	dahnk ü

Note: ü is pronounced as "ee" with lips pursed.

The Dutch usually speak at least one more foreign language in addition to English.

3

GENERAL PROTOCOL & INFORMATION

* The Dutch are very proud of their cultural heritage, technological accomplishments, high standard of living, beautiful country and involvement in international affairs.

* They have a saying: "God made the earth, but the Dutch made Holland."

* Flowers are abundant and the Dutch buy them for their home, as well as office. Dutch flowers are exported all over the world.

CUSTOMER MEETING SCHEDULES
- Common business hours are 8:30 a.m. to 5:00 p.m.

COMMUNICATION DURING CUSTOMER MEETINGS
- Eye contact and facial expressions are important.

- Always identify yourself when initiating or answering a phone call.

DO'S & DONT'S: WORDS AND GESTURES
- A circular motion of the finger around the ear means someone has a phone call. It is the same gesture that in most European and Latin American countries means "crazy."

OTHER USEFUL INFORMATION
- See Western Europe and General Suggestions sections.

3

PORTUGAL

LANGUAGE & KEY WORDS

English	Portuguese (Pronunciation)
Good day	bohn DEE-ah
How are you?	KO-mo ehs-TA
Very well	behn
Happy to meet you	MWEE-toh pra-ZEHR
Goodbye	ah-DEH-ooss
Mr.	sehn-YOR
Mrs.	sehn-YO-ra
Yes	seen
No	nouñ
Excuse me	dehs-KOOL-peh-meh
Please	por fa-VOR
Thank you	oh-bree-GA-doh/ oh-bree-GA-da*

Note: ñ is pronounced as a nasal n.
* Masculine and feminine forms.

GENERAL PROTOCOL & INFORMATION

- Most Portuguese tend to be traditional and conservative. After careful consideration, they will usually accept change and innovation quietly.

- They are very proud of their cultural heritage and economic progress.

INTRODUCTIONS, GREETINGS & BUSINESS CARDS

- A warm and firm handshake is most common. Use a title followed by a surname, although it can be combined with the first name, depending on preference. Use *Senhor, Senhora, Doutor* for anyone you think that might have a university degree, as well as *Engenheiro* and *Arquitecto*, when appropriate.

CUSTOMER MEETING SCHEDULES
- Common business hours are 9 a.m. to 1 p.m. and 3 to 7 p.m.

- Avoid making appointments between noon and 3 p.m. For the Portuguese, it is impressive to arrive on time, but not crucial. They value people and relationships rather than time and would prefer to be late than to end a conversation prematurely. However, it is advisable that you arrive on time.

COMMUNICATION DURING CUSTOMER MEETINGS
- Even though they tend to be reserved, the Portuguese use gestures a great deal.
    - Shaking a pinched earlobe gently while raising the eyebrows means something is really good.
    - Pulling down the skin under the eye with the index finger can indicate that "You are perceptive" or "You are kidding."
    - A common gesture of rubbing the thumb rapidly against the first two fingers indicates money.
    - Rocking the hand with fingers spread and palm down means "more or less."

- Good topics of conversation include family, positive aspects of Portugal and personal interests, but don't be too inquisitive or personal. Avoid talking about politics and government.

DO'S & DON'TS: WORDS & GESTURES
- Don't point an index finger directly at anyone. It is rude.

- To beckon someone, wave all your fingers with the palm facing up.

- Don't make the "V" sign or "rabbit ears" behind anyone's head.

GIFTS
- Not expected.

OTHER USEFUL INFORMATION
- See Western Europe and General Suggestions sections.

SPAIN

LANGUAGE & KEY WORDS

English	Spanish	Pronunciation
Good day	Buenos días	BWEH-nohs DEE-yahs
How are you?	¿Cómo está usted?	KO-mo ess-TA oo-STED
Very well	Muy bien	mwee b'YEN
Happy to meet you	Mucho gusto	MOO-cho GOO-sto
Goodbye	Adiós	ah-d'YOHSS
Mr.	Señor	sen-YOHR
Mrs.	Señora	seh-YO-ra
Yes	Sí	see
No	No	no
Excuse me	Perdón	per-DOHN
Please	Por favor	por fa-VOR
Thank you	Gracias	GRA-s'yahs

3

GENERAL PROTOCOL & INFORMATION

- The Spaniards tend to be friendly, helpful, individualistic and stoic.

- They enjoy conversation and giving advice, often feeling an obligation to correct others' "errors."

- They have a strong sense of personal pride and appearance is very important. Thus, it is important for them to project an image of affluence and social position.

- Regional pride and devotion are strong.

INTRODUCTIONS, GREETINGS & BUSINESS CARDS

- The usual business greeting for both men and women is a handshake. Use a title with the surname. Some people use *Don* and *Doña* with the first name to show special respect.

CUSTOMER MEETING SCHEDULES

- Common business hours are 9 a.m. to 1:30 p.m. & 5 p.m. to 8 p.m.

- Avoid early afternoon meetings. Most offices and shops close for siesta between 1:30 to 4:30 p.m.

COMMUNICATION DURING CUSTOMER MEETINGS

- Most business meetings tend to be informal.

- Procrastination and delay are common due to the Spanish's attempt to cram too many things into too little time. The *mañana* attitude is generally not found in private firms.

- Eye contact is very important.

- Modesty and understatement are highly valued. Assertiveness and boasting are not.

- Technical ability, professionalism and competence don't concern them as much as pride in self-reliance and personal worth.

- They have jokes about other people from other regions of Spain, but self-deprecating humor is rare.

- Good topics of conversation include sports and travel. Avoid talking about religion, family and job.

DO'S & DON'TS: WORDS & GESTURES

- Don't make negative remarks about bullfighting. It is considered more an art than a sport.

- Avoid the OK sign. It is considered obscene. Avoid the "thumb's up" sign as it can be taken as provocative (anywhere except the North) and supportive of the Basque separatist movement.

- Don't yawn or stretch anywhere.

- Women should be aware of eye contact with strangers and new acquaintances, as they might mistake it for interest. Also, don't cross your legs; it is considered to be unlady-like.

GIFTS
- Not expected, but good social gifts include flowers, pastries, cakes and chocolates.

- Don't give dahlias and chrysanthemums (symbols of death).

OTHER USEFUL INFORMATION
- The Spaniards eat dinner later than most people around the world. Restaurants don't usually open until 9 p.m. and is not unusual for them to be full at 11 p.m.

- Read the Western Europe and General Suggestions section.

3

SWEDEN

LANGUAGE & KEY WORDS

English	Swedish (Pronunciation)
Good day	goo dahg
How are you?	hewr stor deh teel
Very well	MEW-ket bra
Happy to meet you	det var ROO-leet
Goodbye	ah-YUH
Mr.	hehrr
Mrs.	frew
Yes	ya
No	ney
Excuse me	fuhr-LOHT
Please	var so good
Thank you	tahk

3

GENERAL PROTOCOL & INFORMATION
• Swedes tend to be reserved but friendly.

• They are proud of their country and its accomplishments. Sweden is one of the most egalitarian societies in the world and has a strong capitalist economy. Taxes are about 50%, down from 70% in 1989.

INTRODUCTIONS, GREETINGS & BUSINESS CARDS
• A hand shake when meeting is common. It is common to address each other by first name, except in formal situations where titles are used. Follow the host's lead.

CUSTOMER MEETING SCHEDULES
• Common business hours are 9 a.m. to 5 p.m. (4 p.m. in summer)

COMMUNICATION DURING CUSTOMER MEETINGS
• Eye contact is important during conversation; however, avoid excessive hand gestures.

- Be careful not to praise another area of Sweden over the one you are visiting, as the Swedes are proud of their towns and regions. Avoid criticizing Swedish culture or politics.

DO'S & DON'TS: WORDS & GESTURES
- Don't litter.

- Good posture is admired.

GIFTS
- Flowers should be taken in odd numbers and unwrapped before presenting them.

OTHER USEFUL INFORMATION
- Swedes appreciate people who know the cultural differences among Sweden, Norway, Denmark and Finland.

- Punctuality is a must when you are invited to a Swedish home. (They serve the meal first vs. starting with pre-dinner cocktails.)

- See Western Europe and General Suggestions sections.

3

SWITZERLAND

LANGUAGE
*   The Swiss usually speak English, in addition to the language of their canton. Those languages are German, French, Italian and Romansch. See Germany, France and Italy for key words.

GENERAL PROTOCOL & INFORMATION
*   Switzerland has three distinct regions: French, German and Italian. Customs of all three cultures are seen.

*   The Swiss value nature, beauty, hard work, sobriety, thrift, independence, tolerance, punctuality, cleanliness, neatness, orderliness and a sense of responsibility.

*   They tend to be conservative and consider it impolite to be a show-off about wealth or anything else.

*   They are proud of their unique system, one that they consider to be ideal and even perfect. Most men serve in the Swiss Army.

*   Switzerland is politically neutral and sponsors the International Red Cross. Its strength derives from its federal system that unites different groups into one country with the motto "Unity, yes; uniformity, no."

INTRODUCTIONS, GREETINGS & BUSINESS CARDS
*   Since Switzerland is multicultural and multilingual, verbal greetings and gestures vary. In international cities like Geneva, English is acceptable and most Swiss do speak English. It is best to greet your customer by title and surname. A handshake for both men and women when meeting and leaving is acceptable.

*   Presenting and exchanging business cards is an important ritual. Bring lots of them.

*   Most Swiss exchange simple greetings in the elevator, even among strangers.

3

CUSTOMER MEETING SCHEDULES
- Common business hours are 8 a.m. to noon & 2 to 6 p.m.

- Punctuality is highly valued. Avoid making appointments during July and August, which tend to be vacation months.

COMMUNICATION DURING CUSTOMER MEETINGS
- An insightful and favorite Swiss saying claims that if someone is late, he is either not wearing a Swiss watch or didn't take a Swiss train.

- Pointing the index finger to your own head to indicate someone is crazy could be taken as a serious insult by some.

- Acceptable topics of conversation include sports, positive experiences in Switzerland, travel and politics. Avoid weight watching and diets (especially during meals) and personal questions (age, job, family or personal life).

DO'S & DON'TS: WORDS & GESTURES
- Don't litter.

- Good posture is admired.

GIFTS
- Flowers should be taken in odd numbers and unwrapped before presenting them.

OTHER USEFUL INFORMATION
- Avoid complaining about your watch being slow. It might be Swiss!

- See Western Europe and General Suggestions sections.

3

UNITED KINGDOM (U.K.)

LANGUAGE
* English is spoken in the U.K., but each country (England, Ireland, Scotland and Wales) has different idioms, as well as accents. Many of the words and idioms could be quite different from those used in the U.S.

GENERAL PROTOCOL & INFORMATION
* The English tend to be formal and conservative. They enjoy traditions and custom. Understatement may give the impression of indifference and coolness. British are suspicious of extremes. They do not appreciate display of emotions or extreme enthusiasm. They prefer to be reserved both on behavior and emotion.

* The British tend to be more class conscious than most Americans.

* Britons are known for their wry sense of humor, which allows them to be self-critical. However, visitors should not take such freedom.

* A person from Scotland is a Scot or Scotsman, not Scotch or Scotchmen.

INTRODUCTIONS, GREETINGS & BUSINESS CARDS
* The British prefer light, nonaggressive handshakes.

* Address people by their titles (Mr., Mrs., Doctor, etc.) plus last name. Most honorary titles (Sir, Dame, and Lord) are used even among acquaintances. Follow others' lead.

* If you want to avoid Americanisms, use "hello" instead of "hi" and don't say "have a nice day" when you leave.

CUSTOMER MEETING SCHEDULES
* Common business hours are 9 a.m. to 5 p.m.

- Appointments are essential; **call or write in advance.** Just showing up is considered impolite. You may be 10 minutes late but not 10 minutes early.

- Avoid making trips to the U.K. in June, July or August, which tend to be vacation months.

COMMUNICATION DURING CUSTOMER MEETINGS
- Meetings tend to be informal in style. They begin and end with social conversations.

- Don't assume that all the participants will be well-prepared or that they have read the agenda. (Bring extra copies and introduce the objectives of the meeting.)

- Emotions are rarely vented and protocol is observed. Conversation tends to be conservative.

- Privacy is valued and expected. The English like to keep their distance during meetings. Avoid excessive hand gestures. Listen carefully and maintain good eye-contact.

- Say "please" and "thank you" as often as it is appropriate.

- British usually end a statement with a question, e.g. "The sky is blue, isn't it?" No answer is expected. Some puzzling British idioms: "He wasn't half angry" means that he was very mad. "It isn't half bad" means that it is very good.

- The British tend to be more subtle and less straightforward than Americans. They are reluctant to be direct for fear of offending anyone.

- Humor is expected and it is important for the British to be entertaining on every possible occasion. However, non-British need not attempt to join in. In fact, it is advisable not to, as humor usually doesn't cross cultures well.

- Avoid talking about politics, royal gossip and religion.

DO'S & DON'TS: WORDS & GESTURES

- Do appreciate that American English is not considered to be the same language as British English.

- Do respect the accomplishments of British technology.

- Avoid any behavior which indicates that British moral superiority is questioned, such as, questioning the assumption that British television is the best in the world and that British weather is the most interesting.

- Avoid striped ties in case they are copies of British regimentals. Avoid asking what the design of a man's tie means, as they are meant to be recognized.

- Avoid shop-talk over drinks or dinner. (When the day is done, so is business.)

- The V sign means victory, but make sure that your palm is facing your audience. (The reverse means, "Up yours!")

- Remove hats when entering a building.

- A nose tap means secrecy or confidentiality.

- In Wales, avoid beckoning to someone with your arms, rubbing your nose and standing with your hands in your pockets or shuffling your feet when you are addressing a group.

GIFTS

- Not expected. Entertainment in the form of a meal, drinks or a night at some cultural event could serve as gifts. Thank you notes are welcome.

- Business gifts should not exceed $15 - $20 to avoid embarrassment.

OTHER USEFUL INFORMATION
- Know the difference between:
    England
    Britain = England, Scotland and Wales, and
    UK = Britain and Northern Ireland

- Remember that English is spoken in England and American is spoken in the U.S. Some English-Americanism include: Lift-elevator, chemist-pharmacist, intercourse-friendly conversation, cookie-biscuit.

- See Western Europe and General Suggestions sections.

3

4

LATIN AMERICA

GENERAL PROTOCOL & INFORMATION

*   If you are *simpático*, you can get away with almost any *faux pas*. Being *simpático* means accepting the Latin ways.

*   Family and personal relationships are highly valued.

*   Machismo is alive and well here. Emotions, especially for men, are much closer to the surface. People converse almost nose-to-nose, eye contact is strong, physical contact is common. Hugs and two-handed handshakes are common even among acquaintances.

INTRODUCTIONS, GREETINGS & BUSINESS CARDS

*   Most people in Latin America use both parents' last names, but usually use only the father's in conversation. In Spanish speak-

ing countries, the father's name comes first. Thus, Enrique Muñoz Samorano is Mr. Muñoz. In Portuguese-speaking Brazil, the mother's last name comes first.

- A warm handshake is the most common greeting, followed by an *abrazo* (a bear hug) among good friends. Address your customer by title (*Señor, Señora* or *Doctor*) and paternal surname in Spanish-speaking countries.

- Bring plenty of business cards; they are always exchanged.

CUSTOMER MEETING SCHEDULES

- Accept that siesta and mañana are often facts of life. Banks and business offices close for two to three hours in the early afternoon. Things get done and people arrive whenever they do.

- Punctuality is not strictly respected. In fact, arriving 15 minutes to an hour late is customary. Plan meetings accordingly.

COMMUNICATION DURING CUSTOMER MEETINGS

- During conversation, personal space tends to be closer than in the U.S. Latins are touch-oriented people.

- Eye contact is very important.

- Patience is a must. Try not to show anger when faced with delays and interruptions.

- Don't start talking about business immediately upon meeting. Most Latins enjoy some light conversation before business. Follow your host's lead.

- Any effort to speak in Spanish is appreciated.

- Say *¡Salud! (good health)* if someone sneezes.

- You might be served small cups of strong coffee.

- "That is a lot" is signaled by whipping the hand and fingers downward with the thumb and forefinger hitting each other.

- Avoid controversial subjects such as politics and religion.

DO'S & DON'TS: WORDS & GESTURES

- There are many gestures used in Latin America. The best thing to do is ask for interpretations if you noticed one that you don't know or understand.

- In Brazil and most of Latin American, avoid the U.S.'s classic OK sign (thumb and forefinger forming a circle with other fingers pointing up), as it conveys the equivalent of the notorious third-finger sign in the U.S. Use the "thumbs up" sign instead.

GIFTS

- Corporate gifts, as discussed in other sections of this Guide, are acceptable.

OTHER USEFUL INFORMATION

- Most Latin Americans are very proud of their children and appreciate your attention paid to them.

4

ARGENTINA

LANGUAGE & KEY WORDS

English	Spanish	Pronunciation
Good day	Buenos días	BWEH-nohs DEE-yahs
How are you?	¿Cómo está usted?	KO-mo ess-TA oo-STED
Very well	Muy bien	mwee b'YEN
Happy to meet you	Mucho gusto	MOO-cho GOO-sto
Goodbye	Adiós	ah-d'YOHSS
Mr.	Señor	sen-YOHR
Mrs.	Señora	seh-YO-ra
Yes	Sí	see
No	No	no
Excuse me	Perdón	per-DOHN
Please	Por favor	por fa-VOR
Thank you	Gracias	GRA-s'yahs

GENERAL PROTOCOL & INFORMATION
- Argentines tend to be very social and friendship plays an important role, especially in business.

- Social and economic standing is valued.

- Argentines have a great deal of respect for the elderly and women (influenced by the Spanish and Italian).

INTRODUCTIONS, GREETINGS & BUSINESS CARDS
- A handshake and a slight nod is common.

CUSTOMER MEETING SCHEDULES
- Common business hours are 9 a.m. to 5 p.m.

COMMUNICATION DURING CUSTOMER MEETINGS
- Wait until your host sits down before sitting.

4

- Argentines tend to touch each other's arm or shoulder, or finger the lapel while conversing.

- Good topics of conversation include soccer and other sports, as well as the beauty of the local parks and gardens.

DO'S & DON'TS: WORDS & GESTURES
- A head tap means "I'm thinking" or "Think."

- Avoid placing hands on the hip. It suggests anger or a challenge.

- Extend the arm with palm down and make a scratching motion to beckon someone.

- There is a strong Italian heritage in Argentina, so many of the Italian gestures apply here.

- To tell someone across the room that they have a phone call, Argentines circle the index finger toward the side of the head (similar to the one that in North America means "You are crazy").

GIFTS
- Avoid personal items.

OTHER USEFUL INFORMATION
- See Latin America and General Suggestions sections.

4

BRAZIL

LANGUAGE & KEY WORDS

English	Portuguese (Pronunciation)
Good day	bohn DEE-ah
How are you?	KO-mo ehs-TA
Very well	behn
Happy to meet you	MWEE-toh pra-ZEHR
Goodbye	ah-DEH-ooss
Mr.	sehn-YOR
Mrs.	sehn-YO-ra
Yes	seen
No	nouñ
Excuse me	dehs-KOOL-peh-meh
Please	por fa-VOR
Thank you	oh-bree-GA-doh/
	oh-bree-GA-da*

*Masculine and feminine forms.
Note: ñ is pronounced as a nasal n.

GENERAL PROTOCOL & INFORMATION
- Brazilians tend to be friendly, warm , free-spirited and outgoing.

- Men stare and make comments about women passing, which the women tend to ignore. This is an acceptable behavior in Brazil.

INTRODUCTIONS, GREETINGS & BUSINESS CARDS
- In Brazil, the mother's last name comes first.

CUSTOMER MEETING SCHEDULES
- Common business hours are 8 a.m. to 6 p.m. (closed 12-2 p.m.)

- Most Brazilians (except those in São Paolo) appear to be casual about time and see it more as a sequence of events instead of hours and minutes.

COMMUNICATION DURING CUSTOMER MEETINGS

- Brazilians tend to be opinionated and argue for their conviction with such forcefulness that it might even appear as anger, which it is not.

- Use the "thumb's up" sign to show approval, not the American "OK" sign, which is an offensive gesture.

- To beckon someone, wave all the fingers on one hand with the palm downward.

- Brazilians say "psssst" to get someone's attention.

- Avoid talking about controversial subjects and asking personal questions, such as salary or age. Don't talk about Argentina.

- Don't speak to a Brazilian in Spanish (unless you have been told that it is OK to do so); English would be preferable. Brazilians are very proud of the fact that Brazil is the only nation in South America whose citizens speak Portuguese.

DO'S & DON'TS: WORDS & GESTURES

- A chin flick means "I don't know."

- The fig (closed fist with index folded over the thumb which is sticking up) is a good luck symbol shown in paper weights and amulets worn around the neck.

- It is vulgar to punch the fist into a cupped hand.

- Don't whistle at people; it is considered rude.

GIFTS

- Avoid purple flowers (symbol of death).

OTHER USEFUL INFORMATION

- Brazilian men enjoy good jokes & laughing, except ethnic jokes.

- See Latin America and General Suggestions sections.

4

CHILE

LANGUAGE & KEY WORDS

English	Spanish	Pronunciation
Good day	Buenos días	BWEH-nohs DEE-yahs
How are you?	¿Cómo está usted?	KO-mo ess-TA oo-STED
Very well	Muy bien	mwee b'YEN
Happy to meet you	Mucho gusto	MOO-cho GOO-sto
Goodbye	Adiós	ah-d'YOHSS
Mr.	Señor	sen-YOHR
Mrs.	Señora	seh-YO-ra
Yes	Sí	see
No	No	no
Excuse me	Perdón	per-DOHN
Please	Por favor	por fa-VOR
Thank you	Gracias	GRA-s'yahs

GENERAL PROTOCOL & INFORMATION

- Chileans are friendly with each other and with strangers.

- They tend to be sharp, pragmatic and have a great sense of humor. Chileans are sometimes called the "British of South America," due to their cultural and educational refinement, as well as wittiness.

- They respect the elderly and the law.

- They are proud of their literacy, heritage and nation.

- They are usually confident and optimistic about Chile and its future.

- There is a strong middle class. Chileans value personal appearance a great deal.

4

INTRODUCTIONS, GREETINGS & BUSINESS CARDS
• Greeting is most important as it reinforces that someone is welcomed and recognized. Professional and social titles (*Doctor, Director, Profesor*) are important. *Don* and *Doña* are used for men and women to show respect and familiarity.

CUSTOMER MEETING SCHEDULES
• Common business hours are 9 a.m. to 6 p.m. Most people take lunch at around 1 or 2 p.m. Dinner is usually after 9 p.m.

• Punctuality is respected. Meetings are usually started and ended on time.

COMMUNICATION DURING CUSTOMER MEETINGS
• Avoid excessive hand gestures.

• Chileans value respect and courtesy.

• Good topics of conversation include: Chile's delicious seafood and beautiful country, especially the Lake District in southern Chile.

DO'S & DON'TS: WORDS & GESTURES
• Chilean idioms, such as, *regio* (great, wonderful) and *al tiro* (immediately) are heard often in conversations.

• Don't beckon anyone with hand gestures, except for waiters.

• Avoid tossing things to others. Instead, hand them over.

4

GIFTS
• Flowers, wine and European chocolates are acceptable.

OTHER USEFUL INFORMATION
• Chile's modern business climate is active and has been most successful in its exports and investment ventures with world partners.

• See Latin America and General Suggestions sections.

MEXICO

LANGUAGE & KEY WORDS

English	Spanish	Pronunciation
Good day	Buenos días	BWEH-nohs DEE-yahs
How are you?	¿Cómo está usted?	KO-mo ess-TA oo-STED
Very well	Muy bien	mwee b'YEN
Happy to meet you	Mucho gusto	MOO-cho GOO-sto
Goodbye	Adiós	ah-d'YOHSS
Mr.	Señor	sen-YOHR
Mrs.	Señora	seh-YO-ra
Yes	Sí	see
No	No	no
Excuse me	Perdón	per-DOHN
Please	Por favor	por fa-VOR
Thank you	Gracias	GRA-s'yahs

GENERAL PROTOCOL & INFORMATION

- Mexicans are proud of their country and history.

- They are friendly, gracious and easygoing.

- Business contacts are often made during a two to three-hour lunch. It usually consists of mostly social discussions with the last few minutes reserved for business.

- Prepare yourself for Mexico City's high altitude, smog and wild traffic and, possibly, "Montezuma's revenge" (diarrhea due to the body's adjustment to the local water).

INTRODUCTIONS, GREETINGS & BUSINESS CARDS

- Greet a woman as *Señorita* (Miss), unless you know for sure that she is married, then address her as *Señora*.

CUSTOMER MEETING SCHEDULES
- Common business hours are 9 a.m. to 6 p.m.

- Mexicans tend to be more casual about time than professionals in the U.S. because they feel that people are more important than schedules (although that is changing).

- If a business associate drops in without an appointment, most Mexicans stop to chat, regardless of how long it takes, even if it makes the person or something else late.

COMMUNICATION DURING CUSTOMER MEETINGS
- Mexicans call citizens of the U.S., *Americanos*, but they love to remind U.S. citizens that Mexico is also in North America. Therefore, they are also Americans.

- "No" can be indicated by shaking the hand side to side with the index finger extended and palm outward.

- "Thumb's up" shows approval.

- Hand and arm gestures are often seen during conversations.

- Good topics for light conversation include weather, fashion, travel, art, Mexico's parks and museums.

DO'S & DON'TS: WORDS & GESTURES
- To show the height of an animal, Mexicans extend the arm out, palm downward to the appropriate height. However, to show people's height, they use a raised index finger.

- Hand, don't toss, things to people.

- Men should not stand with hands in pockets or on hips.

- Avoid placing a "V" made with the index and middle fingers with your palm facing you over your nose. It's a very rude gesture.

4

GIFTS
- Not expected, but appreciated.

- For some Mexicans, yellow flowers are associated with death, red flowers cast spells and white ones lift spells.

OTHER USEFUL INFORMATION
- See the Latin America and General Suggestions sections.

5

MIDDLE EAST

GENERAL PROTOCOL & INFORMATION
- In the Middle East, the Persian Gulf is called the Arabian Gulf. There are over 20 countries in the Middle East, but we will focus on just three for our purpose.

INTRODUCTIONS, GREETINGS & BUSINESS CARDS
- Handshakes are customary, but your host might welcome you with a kiss on both cheeks. You should reciprocate.

- People of the same sex in the Middle East tend to stand and sit closer to each other. Moving away may be interpreted as aloofness. People of the opposite sex tend to stand much farther apart than in the U.S. or Europe.

- Men tend to touch each other a great deal, thus, in addition to the handshake, your Egyptian host might gently touch your elbow with his other hand.

CUSTOMER MEETING SCHEDULES
- Always arrive, but don't expect to leave, on time.

- Plan to conduct business from Saturday to Wednesday or Thursday (the common business week). Thursday and/or Friday is the Muslim day of rest and worship. Also, no work is usually done after noon during Ramadan, the ninth month of the Islamic lunar calendar.

COMMUNICATION DURING CUSTOMER MEETINGS
Some common Arab behaviors include:

- Offering a cup of thick coffee or tea, usually in the beginning of the meeting to establish trust and confidence before moving to business.

- Long and direct eye contact is important for men. Staring is not considered rude.

- To non-Arabs, it appears at times that the Arab eyelids are half closed; this doesn't necessarily indicate disrespect or lack of interest.

- The sincerest form of flattery in the Arab world is to make a graceful religious gesture toward an Arab, such as saying *Inshallah* (God willing), which is used as commonly as OK in the U.S. It can be used as in "See you soon, *Inshallah.*"

- A nonverbal "No" is accomplished by tilting the head backward and either raising the eyebrows or making a clicking sound with the tongue.

- "Thumbs up" usually means "Very good. I am winning."

- Sit properly. Avoid leaning against a wall or standing with your hands in your pockets when talking. It is considered disrespectful.

- Arabs are proud of and enjoy hearing outside acknowledgment of their place in the world economy.

- The Arab's desire to please might lead your partner to say what is agreeable without regard to the truth. They will usually give their word rather than signature to agreements, thus, what seems like a "yes" is really a "no."

- Arab countries also start rather slowly and methodically, similar to the Japanese's getting-acquainted initial meetings. However, be prepared to accept that in the Middle East, your business partners are used to doing business in a communal style, with multiple meetings going on at once. Thus, you might be sharing your host's attention with a stream of people wandering in and out. Plan on meetings that last two to three times as long as you would normally expect. Don't try to rush your customer to stay on your schedule; you will probably achieve the opposite result.

- Muslims pray five times a day. Everything stops during those times, including your meeting. It is best to wait respectfully, without interruption or impatience.

- An Arab is quick to explode at both friend and enemy.

DO'S & DON'TS: WORDS & GESTURES
- Never give, take or eat anything with your left hand. The "unclean" hand is used for body hygiene. Use the right hand for everything else.

- Never show the soles of your shoes to an Arab. Keep your feet flat on the floor or covered, never on a table or crossed over the knee. Shoe soles are the lowest and dirtiest part of the body and, thus, it is rude to point them at anyone.

- Don't walk in front of someone who is praying.

- Don't point with the finger or signal another person with the hand.

- Avoid gesturing with your left hand.

- Pass everything with the right or both hands.

5

GIFTS

- No alcohol.

- Flowers and chocolates are welcome.

OTHER USEFUL INFORMATION

- Many Arabs use "worry beads" to relieve tension. It has nothing to do with religion (most Arabs are Muslim).

- Men: If an Arab takes your hand, either in private or in public, don't get alarmed. It is silent Arabic for friendship and respect.

- Alcohol and pork are forbidden.

- If you don't want your beverage cup refilled, cover it with your hand or shake it gently from side to side several times and say *bes* (enough). Otherwise, an empty cup will be continually filled.

5

EGYPT

LANGUAGE & KEY WORDS

English	Arabic (Pronunciation)
Good day	al sa-lahm a'a-LAY-koom
How are you?	kaif HA-lak / kaif HA-lik*
Very well	mahb-SOOT
Happy to meet you	sa-e'ed BI-le-ka ak / sa-e'ed BE-le-ka ek*
Goodbye	BE-kha trahk
Mr.	sa-YID
Mrs.	sa-YEE-da
Yes	na-a'am
No	la
Excuse me	is-MA-leh
Please	min-FAHD-lak / min-FAHD-lik*
Thank you	shook-RAHN

*Masculine and feminine forms.

GENERAL PROTOCOL & INFORMATION

- *Ma'alesh* , meaning "don't worry", summarizes the relaxed and patient life of Egyptians and is used to dismiss the inevitable, nonserious concerns or conflicts.

- Business, as well as every aspect of life, is governed by a reliance on God, *Inshallah* (God willing), and dominates Muslim life.

- Egypt is community-oriented; personal needs are secondary to the group's.

INTRODUCTIONS, GREETINGS & BUSINESS CARDS

- A light handshake is common. Greetings tend to be expressive and elaborate. Men shake hands with women only if women extend their hand first. Otherwise, a verbal greeting suffices.

5

CUSTOMER MEETING SCHEDULES
- Common business hours are 8:30 a.m. to 1:30 p.m. & 4:30 to 7 p.m. Saturday to Thursday.

- Egyptians tend to be very patient and view events with an extended time frame.

COMMUNICATION DURING CUSTOMER MEETINGS
- Egyptians tend to be expressive and emotional and have a great sense of humor.

- Acceptable topics of conversation include Egyptian achievements, positive reputation of Egypt's leaders, its cotton and ancient civilization. Avoid Middle Eastern politics.

OTHER USEFUL INFORMATION
- A beard can be a sign of religious faith and can also express political membership.

- See Middle East and General Suggestions sections.

5

ISRAEL

LANGUAGE & KEY WORDS

English	Hebrew (Pronunciation)
Good day	sha-LOHM
How are you?	ma-shlohm-KHAH / ma-shlo-MEKH*
Very well	tohv meh-OHD
Happy to meet you	na-EEM lee meh-OHD
Goodbye	sha-LOHM
Mr.	ah-DOHN
Mrs.	GVEH-ret
Yes	kehn
No	lo
Excuse me	tis-LAHKH-lee
Please	beh-va-ka-SHA
Thank you	toh DAH

Note: Hebrew is written from right to left.
*Masculine and feminine forms.

GENERAL PROTOCOL & INFORMATION

- Israelis tend to be very informal, and titles are even less important than in the U.S.

- Israel is surrounded by Arab countries, but their customs are likely to be very different from its neighbors.

- Israelis are devoted to their culture and state.

- "Jewish" doesn't describe an ethnic group or population, but a religion and a culture uniting the Jews from around the world.

- Sabbath (Saturday) is observed from Friday nightfall to Saturday nightfall.

5

INTRODUCTIONS, GREETINGS & BUSINESS CARDS
- Informal greetings and a handshake are common. Shalom (peace) is the usual greeting upon meeting and departing. Don't be surprised if you are addressed by your first name.

CUSTOMER MEETING SCHEDULES
- Common business hours are 8 a.m. to 1 p.m. & 4 to 7 p.m. (Sunday through Thursday).

- Be punctual, as Israelis tend to be time-conscious.

COMMUNICATION DURING CUSTOMER MEETINGS
- Israelis are inquisitive and appreciate those who take an interest in them. Avoid talking about religion and U.S. aid.

- Some Israelis are very expressive with their hands and bodies; others are not.

- Israelis tend to stand quite close to each other during conversations. Don't be surprised if your host touches your arm while speaking.

- If you see someone point down the forefinger of one hand at the upturned palm of the other hand, beware. It is an insult meaning "grass will grow on my hand" before the speaker's comments come true.

- The U.S. OK sign and "thumbs up" mean OK; V means victory.

GIFTS
- Books are good choices, as most Israelis enjoy reading a great deal.

OTHER USEFUL INFORMATION
- State law requires that workers get at least one day off: Fridays for Muslims, Saturdays for Jews and Sundays for Christians.

- See Middle East and General Suggestions sections.

5

SAUDI ARABIA

LANGUAGE & KEY WORDS

English	Arabic (Pronunciation)
Good day	al sa-lahm a'a-LAY-koom
How are you?	kaif HA-lak / kaif HA-lik*
Very well	mahb-SOOT
Happy to meet you	sa-e'ed BI-le-ka ak / sa-e'ed BE-le-ka ek*
Goodbye	BE-kha trahk
Mr.	sa-YID
Mrs.	sa-YEE-da
Yes	na-a'am
No	la
Excuse me	is-MA-leh
Please	min-FAHD-lak / min-FAHD-lik*
Thank you	shook-RAHN

*Masculine and feminine forms.

GENERAL PROTOCOL & INFORMATION

- Life in Saudi Arabia tends to be relatively relaxed and conservative.

- Saudi Arabians take time to establish trust and confidence before talking business. They also tend to be generous.

- Because family, honor (personal and family) and privacy are important to them, Saudi Arabians can be easily offended if they perceive an insult in any of those areas.

- Saudi Arabians are very religious and Islamic customs play a key role in their cultural practices.

- They are also very patriotic and proud of their modern country.

5

INTRODUCTIONS, GREETINGS & BUSINESS CARDS
- A Saudi's elaborate greeting begins with saying *salaam alaykum* and shaking hands, often extending his left hand to your right shoulder and kissing you on both cheeks. Thereafter, he might take your hand in his, as a sign of kinship.

CUSTOMER MEETING SCHEDULES
- Common business hours are 8 a.m. to noon & 5 to 8 p.m. (Saturday to Wednesday).

- Punctuality is appreciated. There might be other business people present. Several meetings may occur simultaneously, with people coming in and out of the room. Expect interruptions and plan your meetings accordingly.

- Office hours are in the evening and extend past midnight during Ramadan, but it's preferable to schedule your visit before or after Ramadan.

COMMUNICATION DURING CUSTOMER MEETINGS
- The importance of eye contact can be summarized by the saying "the eyes are the windows to the soul."

- "Yes" can be indicated by swiveling the head from side to side.

- When a Saudi loses interest toward the end of the meeting, he might direct the conversation to nonbusiness matters.

- Avoid talking about Middle Eastern and international oil politics.

DO'S & DON'TS: WORDS & GESTURES
- Don't ask about your host's wife.

- Don't over-admire your host's possessions; he might give them to you and will be offended if you don't accept them.

- Don't be surprised nor pull your hand away sharply if an Arab businessman takes your hand and holds it while walking. This is simply a sign of friendship.

5

GIFTS
- First time visitors shouldn't give a gift to the woman of the house.

- Don't give any items prohibited by Islam, e.g., photos and sculptures of women.

OTHER USEFUL INFORMATION
- Friday is the Muslim day of worship when men go to the mosque to pray and hear recitations from the Qur'an. Women pray at home.

- Women are forbidden to drive cars or ride bicycles.

- Don't expect to be introduced to the woman accompanying your host.

- If you don't want your beverage cup refilled, cover it with your hand or shake it gently from side to side several times and say *bes* (enough). Otherwise, an empty cup will be continually filled.

5

6

U.S.A., Canada & Australia

GENERAL PROTOCOL & INFORMATION
- The three countries grouped together in this section tend to have much in common in their communication styles and business etiquette.

INTRODUCTIONS, GREETINGS & BUSINESS CARDS
- A firm handshake accompanied by a greeting with the customer's title and surname is common.

- Business cards are usually exchanged.

CUSTOMER MEETING SCHEDULES
• Scheduled appointments and punctuality are a must.

COMMUNICATION DURING CUSTOMER MEETINGS
• Eye contact is important.

• Be concise and to the point. Time is of the essence.

GIFTS
• Not expected, but appreciated. Follow the General Suggestions and those shown in the next few pages.

6

UNITED STATES OF AMERICA (U.S.)

LANGUAGE
* English is the official language. Most U.S.-born speak only English, but immigrants and their children tend to speak their native language as well.

GENERAL PROTOCOL & INFORMATION
* Americans tend to be outspoken, frank and appreciative of candidness.

* They value innovation, industry, integrity, individualism, entrepreneurship, freedom and independence (both for the nation and the individual).

* They appreciate a good sense of humor, and can usually laugh at themselves and others.

* They are very proud of their country and, even though they openly criticize their government, most are patriotic and believe that the U.S. is one of the greatest countries in the world.

* Americans have come from everywhere in the world, which provides a great deal of cultural diversity and social challenges.

INTRODUCTION, GREETING & BUSINESS CARD
* Use firm handshakes for both men and women. Using a title (Ms., Mrs., Dr., Mr.) with the surname shows respect, although most people do go by their first name after the initial introduction, especially in the West. There are regional differences, including *Aloha* in Hawaii, but *Hello* and *Hi* are acceptable. When Americans greet each other with *How are you?*, a *Fine, thanks* is the expected answer.

* People usually exchange business cards. It is common, while not acceptable, for some people to take your card and put it in their pocket without reading it. The business card ritual is quick and simple without much ceremony.

6

CUSTOMER MEETING SCHEDULES

- Common business hours are 9 a.m. to 5 p.m .

- Americans tend to be most time-conscious and meetings are expected to begin and end on time.

COMMUNICATION DURING CUSTOMER MEETINGS

- Americans like to keep an arm's-length distance while conversing.

- Direct eye contact, not staring, is crucial to show your interest, sincerity and trustworthiness.

- Americans are uncomfortable with silence and will try to quickly fill it with conversation.

- Don't be surprised if your host is a woman. Women professionals and business owners are quite common. It is best to talk with them as you would with a male host.

- It is acceptable to point, using the index finger.

- Both the commonly seen "thumb's up" and OK gestures are acceptable.

- To beckon, Americans wave the index finger or all the fingers with the palm facing up.

- Americans are casual, including the way they sit (legs apart, feet up on chairs or placing an ankle from one leg on the other knee). Poor posture is not appropriate, but common.

- Don't discuss extremely personal questions, especially with women (including marital status). If she is married, you might casually inquire about her children and her husband's occupation.

DO'S & DON'TS: WORDS & GESTURES

- Do leave messages in telephone answering machines and voice

6

mail systems. Electronic mail systems are becoming popular, even outside of the high technology industries.

- Don't pat anyone's rear end. Avoid other questionable or potentially offensive physical contact.

- Avoid the middle finger thrust and the forearm jerk; they are both rude and insulting.

GIFTS
- Acceptable are items of quality but not overly expensive ones for the office, or something from your home country.

- Avoid personal gifts. Don't be offended if Americans don't reciprocate immediately with a gift in return. They might wait until you arrive home or when you return next time to present you with a small gift or some entertainment.

- Gifts are commonly opened in front of the giver to express appreciation.

OTHER USEFUL INFORMATION
- Most U.S. offices are designated nonsmoking areas but may have some designated smoking areas. In all cases, ask permission before smoking if you are with others. People expect the "No Smoking" rule to be respected.

- It is common to put on the announcement both the starting and ending times for meetings, parties and events. Those times are to be respected.

- Good luck is gestured by crossing the middle finger over the forefinger. Winking can mean flirtation, friendliness, amusement or "I'm just kidding."

- To say good-bye, most people move the open hand from side to side or shake hands.

- See the U.S.A., Canada & Australia section and the General Suggestions section.

6

CANADA

LANGUAGE
- Both English and French are the official languages. In certain part of Québec, French is used exclusively.

GENERAL PROTOCOL & INFORMATION
- Canadians tend to be open and friendly.

- Politeness and etiquette are highly valued.

- Canadians are proud of their cultural heritage (French, British and other European influences).

- While there are many similarities between the U.S. and Canada, Canadians resent being treated as U.S. citizens living in Canada.

- Preservation of the Canadian culture, especially in Québec, is very important in Canada. For many people in Québec, Québec *is* Canada.

- Atlantic Canadians tend to be more conservative and traditional, as well as very patriotic.

- Some facts that Canadians appreciate: Canada is the second largest country in the world and is the U.S.'s largest trading partner.

INTRODUCTION, GREETING & BUSINESS CARD
- Greetings vary in language and style, depending on the region.

- French-speaking Canadians tend to be more open and outgoing than those of British ancestry. Follow your host's lead.

CUSTOMER MEETING SCHEDULES
- Common business hours are 9 a.m. to 5 p.m.

6

COMMUNICATION DURING CUSTOMER MEETINGS
- Eye contact is important.

- Most gestures are similar to the ones in the U.S. (See U.S. sections.) However, there are regional differences.

- Burping in public is offensive, even if you excuse yourself.

- Don't use the American "thumb's down" (no or bad) in Québec; it's offensive.

- Avoid taking sides on partition (dividing Canada into French and English-speaking Canada).

OTHER USEFUL INFORMATION
- See the U.S.A., Canada & Australia section and General Suggestions section.

6

AUSTRALIA

LANGUAGE
* English is the official language.

GENERAL PROTOCOL & INFORMATION
* Australians are friendly and easy going, as well as direct and informal. They usually tell it like it is.

* They dislike overly expressive behaviors.

* They resent those who attempt to pull rank. They have a strong sense of community and value collective effort.

INTRODUCTIONS, GREETINGS & BUSINESS CARDS
* Men often call their friends "mate."

CUSTOMER MEETING SCHEDULES
* Common business hours are 8:30 a.m. to 5 p.m.

COMMUNICATION DURING CUSTOMER MEETINGS
* Rules of etiquette are followed.

* Winking at women is inappropriate.

* Most gestures are similar to the ones in North America, but flashing the V sign with palm facing in and "thumb's up" are considered inappropriate.

* Australian idioms include:
    spot on = right on
    dinky-ki = genuine

* Visitors should use standard English, rather than local slang.

6

DO'S & DON'TS: WORDS & GESTURES

- Do not litter. Australians have a high standard of cleanliness.

- Avoid sniffling in public, even if you have a cold. Blow your nose in private.

OTHER USEFUL INFORMATION

- See the U.S.A., Canada and Australia Summary section and the General Suggestion section.

6

III

APPENDIX

WHAT TO KNOW BEFORE YOU GO
(OR BEFORE YOUR CUSTOMERS ARRIVE)

Ten Tips To Communicating Effectively With Customers Around The World

❑ **1. Keys to Success: Observe, listen and speak,** in that order. Keep an open mind and show respect.

❑ **2. Do Your Homework:** Get briefed on "must-know" information, e.g., current business etiquette, cultural and customer values/sensitivities, communication do's and don'ts, current events and relevant history.

❑ **3. When and Why Meet:** Avoid dates on or around national holidays or vacation. Reconfirm date, time, objective, agenda and people involved in meeting.

❑ **4. Language:** Learn to say a few words in your customers' language, such as, "Hello", "Thank you", "Please" and "Excuse me. " Bring your own interpreter.

❑ **5. Business Cards:** Bring lots of business cards - printed in both the local language and English.

❑ **6. Introductions and Greetings:** Use customers' last name, not their first name unless invited to. If unsure, ask how they would like to be addressed. Speak, act and dress more formally and conservatively.

❑ **7. Communication Do's:**
- Take time to create rapport and trust. Most people prefer to do business with friends.
- Be sensitive to eye contact level, physical distance, time and other non-verbal clues.
- Avoid "or" and judgmental questions.

❑ **8. Communication Don'ts:**
- Avoid discussing politics, religion and social conditions.
- Avoid the U.S. "OK" sign.
- Avoid copying local gestures unless you are sure about their meanings and exact movements.

❑ **9. Business Gifts:** Pens, books, and quality items with a small corporate logo are usually "safe" gifts.

❑ **10. When In Doubt:** Follow your customers' or local staff's lead.

INTERNATIONAL CUSTOMER MEETING CHECKLIST

Below are some activities for you to consider for a productive cross cultural customer meeting:

☐ Do pre-meeting actions items, e.g., sending a confirmation letter with discussion items.

☐ Review and take along sections from *Communicating With Customers Around The World* with suggestions for the region and the country in which you will be conducting your meeting. You might also want to review the General Suggestions and the rest of this checklist.

☐ Confirm with one of your local staff or contacts the relevance of the suggestions you have, as they apply to the customer you will be visiting.

☐ Get an update and briefing from your local staff or someone who is familiar with the country, on additional business etiquette, communication do's and don'ts and cultural sensitivities.

☐ Meet with your customer meeting team, if relevant, on the necessary preparation for your international customer visits.

☐ Reconfirm with the customer and local staff or contact the date, time, objective, agenda and people involved in each customer meeting. Reconfirm that it is not on or around a holiday.

☐ Confirm that one of your local company representatives or an interpreter hired by your company will be at the meeting. Meet with him/her before the customer meeting to clarify the objectives and agenda.

☐ Read about the culture and history of the country you plan to visit. See the resource list.

❏ Learn a few key words; see the Language & Key Words section for each country.

❏ Bring lots of business cards. Have them printed in both the local language and English, especially for Asian customer meetings.

❏ Ask your customers how they would like to be addressed. Dress, speak and act more conservatively and formally than you might in your home country.

❏ Remember to create rapport and to probe during the customer meeting, as appropriate. Be sensitive to the level of eye contact, physical distance, time and other nonverbal communication.

❏ Bring business gifts, if appropriate. Check with your local staff or business partner.

❏ When in doubt, follow your host's or local staff's lead. Ask non-judgmental questions.

❏ Keep an open mind and show respect toward your customers.

❏ Get plenty of rest and enjoy your visit. International customer meetings demand more energy and alertness.

❏ Send to the author anecdotes, informative or interesting suggestions and lessons learned from your international customer meetings.

CROSS-CULTURAL COMMUNICATION RESOURCES

We hope that these recommended books will help make your communication and interactions with international customers and business partners more productive and enjoyable. Many of them were reviewed in the development of this book. This is a selected list. If you encounter other valuable resources or have comments about the ones here, let us know. Happy Cross-Cultural Communicating!

Ames, Helen Wattley. Spain Is Different. Intercultural Press, Yarmouth, Maine, 1992.

Axtell, Roger. *Do's And Taboos Around The World*. Wiley & Son, New York, 1990.

Axtell, Roger. *Gestures: The Do's And Taboos of Body Language Around the World*. Wiley & Son, New York, 1991.

Berlitz, Charles. *Around The World With 80 Words*. Putnam Publishing Group, New York, 1991.

Bragnati, Nancy & Devine, Elizabeth. *European Customs And Manners*. Meadowbrook, Minnesota, 1992.

Brannen, Christalyn. *Going to Japan on Business: A Quick Guide To Protocol, Travel, And Language*. Stone Bridge Press, Berkeley, California, 1990.

Brannen, Christalyn & Wilen, Tracy. *Doing Business With Japanese Men: A Woman's Handbook*. Stone Bridge Press, Berkeley, California, 1993.

Brislin, Richard. *Intercultural Interactions: A Practical Guide*. Sage, California, 1986.

Carroll, Raymonde. *Cultural Misunderstandings: The French-American Experience.* University of Chicago, Illinois, 1990.

Chambers, Kevin. *Asian Customs & Manners.* Meadowbrook, Minnesota, 1988.

Chan-Herur, K. C. *Communicating With Customers Around The World.* AuMonde International, San Francisco, 1994.

Chan-Herur, K. C. *Cross-Cultural Power & Influence: The Art of Getting Things Done Across Cultures.* AuMonde International, San Francisco, 1996. If you would like advanced preliminary findings, please contact the author at Geneva Consulting Group, San Francisco, California (415/ 979.5574).

Chang, Jung. *Wild Swans: Three Daughters Of China.* Flamingo, London, 1993.

Condon, John & Yousef, Fathi. *An Introduction To Intercultural Communication.* MacMillan Publishing, New York, 1975.

Condon, John. *Good Neighbors: Communicating With The Mexicans.* Intercultural Press, Yarmouth, Maine, 1985.

Copeland, Lennie & Griggs, Lewis. *Going International.* Random House, New York, 1985.

David M. Kennedy Center for International Studies. *Culturgram.* Brigham Young University, Salt Lake City, Utah, 1992.

De Mente, Boye. *Japanese Etiquette & Ethics In Business.* NTC Business Books, Chicago, IL, 1987.

De Mente, Boye. *Korean Etiquette & Ethics In Business.* NTC Business Books, Chicago, IL, 1988.

Hall, Edward. *The Hidden Dimension.* Doubleday, New York, 1966.

Hall, Edward. *The Silent Language*. Doubleday, New York, 1959.

Hall, Edward & Hall, Mildred Reed. *Understanding Cultural Differences: Germans, French And Americans*. Intercultural Press, Yarmouth, Maine, 1990.

Harris, Phillip & Moran, Robert. *Managing Cultural Differences*. Gulf Publishing, Houston, Texas, 1987.

Kohls, Robert. *Survival Kit For Overseas Living*. Intercultural Press, Yarmouth, Maine, 1984.

Macleod, Roderick. *China Inc.: How To Do Business With The Chinese*. Bantam, New York, 1988.

Marshall, Terry. *The Whole World Guide To Language Learning*. Intercultural Press, Yarmouth, Maine, 1989.

Mole, John. *When In Rome. . . A Business Guide To Cultures & Customs In 12 European Nations*. Amacom, New York, 1991.

Moran, Robert & Stripp, William. *Successful International Business Negotiations*. Gulf Publishing, Houston, 1991.

Nydell, Margaret. *Understanding Arabs*. Intercultural Press, Yarmouth, Maine, 1987.

Renwick, George. *A Fair Go For All: Australian / American Interactions*. Intercultural Press, Yarmouth, Maine, 1991.

Richmond, Yale. *From Nyet To Da: Understanding The Russians*. Intercultural Press, Yarmouth, Maine, 1992.

Salzman, Mark. *Iron & Silk*. Vintage Departures, New York, 1990.

Seligman, Scott. *Dealing With The Chinese*. Warner, New York, 1989.

Smith, Hendrick. *The New Russians*. Avon Books, New York, 1991.

Storti, Craig. *Cross-Cultural Dialogues*. Intercultural Press, Yarmouth, Maine, 1994.

Samovar, Larry & Porter, Richard. *Intercultural Communication: A Reader*. Wadsworth, 1994.

Walmsley, Jane. *Brit-Think, Ameri-Think*. Penguin Books, New York and London, 1987.

Publishers Of Cross-Cultural Books:

Intercultural Press, Yarmouth, Maine, specializes in books on cross-cultural communication and international subjects. Two valuable series are: *Update* and *InterAct*. *Update* provides the latest information about living in a particular country and *InterAct* focuses on communication between two cultures.

Graphics Arts Center Publishing Company, Portland, Oregon, has an excellent series called *Culture Shock!* , which provides information about living in many countries around the world.

Barron's Educational Services, New York, New York, has an informative series called Barron's Bilingual Business Guide: *Talking Business In French/ German/ Japanese/ Korean/ Spanish, etc.*

A SPEAKER ON GLOBAL SUCCESS
WITH GLOBAL EXPERIENCE

K. C. Chan-Herur is a popular speaker and trainer at corporations, professional organizations and universities.

Ms. Chan-Herur's speeches & training programs for corporations and professional associations include:

☐ Global Success: Communicating Effectively With Customers Around The World

☐ Succeeding In International Marketing And Sales

☐ Bridging The Gap: Speaking Effectively To An International Audience

☐ The Art of Getting Things Done Across Cultures: Cross-Cultural Power & Influence

☐ Communicating Across Cultures (International and in the U.S.A.)

"Dynamic! . . . Practical! . . . Informative!"
are typical adjectives that audiences use to describe
K. C. Chan-Herur

To make your global meetings a success, please contact:
K. C. Chan-Herur
Geneva Consulting Group
P.O. Box 471688
San Francisco, Ca 94147-1688
Phone: 415. 979.5574
Fax: 415. 771.7731
E-mail: 71514.3310@CompuServe.COM

ABOUT THE AUTHOR

K. C. Chan-Herur, MBA, is a professional speaker, author and principal of Geneva Consulting Group, a San Francisco-based company providing training and resources vital for successful international business communication and marketing. Her 15 years of Fortune 500 marketing management, communication and consulting experience in the U.S. and internationally ranges from Procter & Gamble, Nestlé to Sun Microsystems and from Apple Computer to American Express.

Ms. Chan-Herur received a Master of Business Administration from The Wharton School, University of Pennsylvania, and a Bachelor of Science in Civil Engineering from the University of California, Berkeley.

This "global citizen" has had over 25 years of cross-cultural living and business experience across four continents. She grew up in Macau, Hong Kong, Chile and the U. S. A. Ms. Chan-Herur speaks English, Spanish, French and Chinese. Her interest in international business and culture prompted her to work, study and travel in more than twenty countries in Europe and the Pacific Rim region in the last 15 years.

Ms. Chan-Herur is on the faculty of the University of California, Berkeley Extension and teaches at the University of San Francisco. She is the author of *Communicating With Customers Around The World: A Practical Guide To Effective Cross-Cultural Business Communication* (AuMonde International, San Francisco). Her current research and book-in-progress, *Cross-Cultural Power and Influence: The Art of Getting Things Done Across Cultures*, is scheduled for publication by AuMonde International in 1996.

HOW TO GET YOUR COPY OF
Communicating With Customers Around The World
ISBN 1-885269-18-8

Check with your local bookstores. If you are unable to purchase it locally, you can order it directly by using the form below:

PLEASE PRINT

Name _____

Title_____

Organization _____

Address_____

State _____ Zip _____ Country _____

Phone (   ) _____ Fax (   )_____

E-Mail _____

How did you hear about this book?_____

Please send me ____copies X **$12.95** $ _____
plus Shipping & Handling: _____
Within U.S.A. - $3.00 first copy, $1.00 additional copy
Outside of U.S.A - $6.00 per copy
Tax: California residents add 8.5 % sales tax   _____

                                   Total $ _____

Form Of Payment:
❑ **Check** (drawn on U.S. banks) or **International Money Order**
❑ **American Express** (Order to be sent to billing address only)
    Card Number _____
    Expiration Date _____
    Cardholder Signature _____

AuMonde International Publishing Company
P.O. Box 471705, San Francisco, CA 94147-1705, U.S.A.
Tel: 415. 281. 8470   Fax: 415. 771. 7731

For Corporate / Volume Purchases, Please Call Us.

HOW TO GET YOUR COPY OF
Communicating With Customers Around The World
ISBN 1-885269-18-8

Check with your local bookstores. If you are unable to purchase it locally, you can order it directly by using the form below:

PLEASE PRINT

Name_____

Title_____

Organization _____

Address_____

State_____ Zip _____ Country _____

Phone (   )_____ Fax (   )_____

E-Mail _____

How did you hear about this book?_____

Please send me ____copies X **$12.95** $ _____
plus Shipping & Handling: _____
Within U.S.A. - $3.00 first copy, $1.00 additional copy
Outside of U.S.A - $6.00 per copy
Tax: California residents add 8.5 % sales tax   _____

                                     Total $ _____

Form Of Payment:
☐ **Check** (drawn on U.S. banks) or **International Money Order**
☐ **American Express** (Order to be sent to billing address only)
    Card Number _____
    Expiration Date_____
    Cardholder Signature _____

AuMonde International Publishing Company
P.O. Box 471705, San Francisco, CA 94147-1705, U.S.A.
Tel: 415. 281. 8470   Fax: 415. 771. 7731

For Corporate / Volume Purchases, Please Call Us.